D1002489

YOU'RE MORE THAN A DIVERSITY HIRE®
WOMEN IN STEM

You're More Than a Diversity Hire®

WOMEN IN STEM

The Five Keys to Unlocking Your Full Potential

Angelique Adams, PhD

© Copyright 2020 by Angelique Adams, PhD

Print ISBN: 978-1-7360644-0-5 | eBook ISBN: 978-1-7360644-1-2

Editor: Kimberley Lim

Designer: Sarah Beaudin

Author photo: David Santos

For more information, email angelique@drangeliqueadams.com.

GET YOUR FREE GIFT!

YOU'RE MORE THAN A DIVERSITY HIRE®
WOMEN IN STEM WORKBOOK

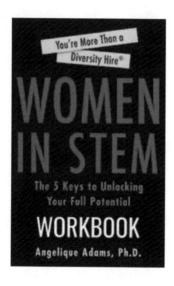

To get the best experience with this book,
I've found readers who download and use the
*You're More than A Diversity Hire®: Women in STEM
Workbook* are able to implement these lessons faster and
take the next steps needed to jump-start their careers.

You can get a free copy by visiting:
https://pages.drangeliqueadams.com/wisworkbook

For Seth and Sophia.

My daily inspiration is to make you proud of me.

CONTENTS

PREFACE

In 2018, I snapped this selfie outside of a bathroom. I was in a manufacturing facility in a remote location in the Middle East. There were no women employees, and women visitors were so rare that there were no ladies' restrooms; they had to make one for me. To me, this symbolized the dilemma of my career: loving what I do but not always feeling like I belong. Sometimes I feel like I am just a visitor. I've been accused of only being a diversity hire. I've been mistaken for the laboratory assistant. I've had my ideas stolen in meetings. I've been excluded from social events with my male colleagues, just to name a few.

While I was getting my executive MBA at the Massachusetts Institute of Technology (MIT), I shared my feelings of self-doubt and frustration with my classmates. They encouraged me to tell my story and share my wisdom with others. But having a sample size of one didn't sit well with me. I am a scientist after all. So, I decided to collect more data—and the Lady Visitor project was born.

It started out with me interviewing a few women whom I already knew. Then it grew. Any time I mentioned my project to someone, a conversation started. All of the women who worked in male-dominated fields had a story to tell. They've been assumed to be the staff assistant or a teaching assistant. They've been judged harshly by their male colleagues for getting to where they are for reasons other than their merits. They've been judged by staff at their kids' preschools for not being the one to pick up their child every day. The men I knew all made recommendations and referrals of women whom they respected. I started a website to collect input from women who were interested in the topic. I eventually started a private LinkedIn community that now has over eighty members.

Below are the original interview questions. My favorite is #10—I call it "Jessica's question." When I went to my local web-design shop, Jessica was assigned to my project. When I told her what I was doing, she immediately launched into a story about how when people walk into the store and see her, they often automatically assume that she is the receptionist, not the developer. So I started asking that question, and 100 percent of the women I talked to had a similar story. We have been mistaken for receptionists, assistants, and flight attendants.

The Original Lady Visitor Project Survey

1. You chose this line of work even though you knew it was going to be a challenge. What do you love most about?

2. What exciting new things are happening in your field?

3. What is next for you, personally?

4. What does achieving that next step mean for you?

5. I would love to get your advice for women who are just starting out. If you think back five years ago, what were you most worried about in your career, and how did you overcome it?

6. Do you think you missed out on anything while you were trying to figure this out?

7. Was there anything that your organization could have done to help you?

8. What about now—you are obviously so capable, having made it this far—what do you think is holding you back from getting to your next goal?

9. Is there anything you are missing out on?

10. Every woman I have talked to so far has her version of the "I went to an important meeting and they assumed I was the assistant." Do you have a story about being the only woman in the room?

Eventually, after dozens of interviews of women in a wide range of STEM- related fields such as academia, research, manufacturing and product development, I thought I might have enough material for a book. And somehow, I had the crazy idea that I could write it.

I know, there's no shortage of books about women in the workplace. At the time of this writing, an Amazon.com search showed over sixty thousand books in the "business books for women" category, and over four thousand books in the "career development for women" category. I won't claim to have read them all. Of the ones I have read, they have failed to address the unique circumstances of women who have chosen to pursue careers in male-dominated STEM workplaces.

Photo courtesy of Lauren Dryer, 2018

PROBLEM NUMBER ONE: Many books are about women in the workplace in general. Any book that focuses on how to dress and apply makeup or how to stand with the right posture (you know, power posing) doesn't get how we spend our days: behind a computer screen, in a lab coat and safety glasses, or in a hard hat and steel-toed boots. Don't get me wrong, I am not saying that women in STEM fields don't dress up and wear makeup. What I am saying is that oftentimes this isn't what our day-to-day life is like, so the advice on these topics isn't relevant.

PROBLEM NUMBER TWO: Many of the books were written by academics who study women like us through interviews and surveys. I have been among the "subjects" of at least half a dozen of these studies. I fill out surveys and participate in focus groups. Yes, I get interrupted all the time. Yes, it would be great if I had someone championing my career. Blah, blah, blah …

While there can be useful information in those books, they generally fall short because they are asking superficial questions and we are giving them superficial answers.

I know this because when I started asking questions, I got answers that I had never read about before. Like the numerous women who told me they went into science not because they loved it but because they desperately wanted to have a job that earned enough so they wouldn't have to rely on a man. Or the woman who shared that her boss gave her a hundred dollars and told her to take the staff assistant to go pick out something suitable to wear to the awards ceremony (in other words, a dress). Or the woman who had to put up with men congregating outside her breast-milk-pumping room (a.k.a. the supply closet) to heckle her when she left (wait, that is my story).

We don't tell academics this stuff because we don't trust them. I know I never said anything. We have the sense that they aren't really trying to help us. They are trying to get more research dollars, which means they have to summarize the information and use it to confirm a research question. Then they have to repackage it so the business consultants of the world can turn it into a training program and sell it.

I hope the women who contributed to this book feel that I have represented their perspectives well. All of the concepts in this book come from their ideas. All the quotes, unless specified otherwise, come from the women I have interviewed or who have engaged in the Lady Visitor Project online community.

The phrase "More than a Diversity Hire®" came from a discussion with my husband. He wanted my advice about something, but he was very nervous to ask me, which is strange. He described the scenario: He knows that his workplace is lacking diversity, especially with respect to women and people of color. He knew a professor at a historically Black college who was doing some interesting work in a related field. My husband wanted to reach out to him to see if they could collaborate to build a more diverse pipeline of postdocs. But he was hesitant. He didn't want to seem like he was jumping on the diversity bandwagon. He didn't want to insult the professor.

I asked him a few questions:
- Does the professor's work line up with your own? Yes.
- Is the work well respected in the field? Yes.
- Do you think that the postdoctoral researchers could contribute to the mission of your group? Yes.
- So, you see this as more than a diversity hire? Yes!

"Okay, then put all of that in the introduction to your email," I advised him. "If you can demonstrate that you respect his work and his students, then I don't think you can go wrong with 'cold-calling' him."

That night and for the next week, I couldn't get the phrase "more than a diversity hire" out of my mind. Then I tested it with my Lady Visitor Project LinkedIn community. It resonated with so many of them who have, along the way, got the message that they were only the diversity hire. So, I wanted to write a book to help them see that they are more than that.

You are more than that.

You're more than a diversity hire.

INTRODUCTION

You chose a STEM career for a reason. Maybe you were good at math and science in school, or you had a great role model, or you wanted a good job with an attractive starting salary. Whatever your motivation for starting this journey, now you want more. You want to make a significant impact in your chosen field. You want to earn the respect and salary you deserve. You want to do all those things for the people and the projects that you care about the most without sacrificing time.

But you are stuck.

You might be just starting out and realizing that full-time work is nothing like your internship. You might have been working for a few years, got off the fast track to start a family, and returned only to find that your organization has left you behind. Maybe you have reached a career plateau and can't figure out what you need to do to move forward. Or maybe you have the dream job but still feel frustrated. Everything seems so much harder for you than your male colleagues, and you feel guilty that it takes all of your energy just to keep your head above water.

Does this sound familiar?

I get it. I have been there. I am an engineer with over twenty-five years of experience in some of the world's most male-dominated workplaces, including oil and gas, metals and mining, and tech. Most recently, I served as the chief innovation officer for a multibillion-dollar manufacturer of steel. I have spent most of my career as the only woman in the room.

Overall, I have loved my career. I like to solve complex problems, I like to create things, and frankly, I like the salary. But there have been times when I've felt as if I didn't belong.

I can tell you, you are not alone in your feelings of frustration and self-doubt. The obstacles holding women like us back are very real. Near-constant messages that we didn't earn our places based on our merits. That we are "diversity hires." Colleagues who don't acknowledge our contributions. Sometimes they even steal our ideas. Our organizations don't help us move forward. The system is opaque, and we can't always find the resources we need to chart our career path. Friends and even our own family sometimes judge us for choosing to work hard on our career.

Like you, with all these challenges, eventually I really started to question myself. I wondered if I could succeed to the level I thought I was capable of and to the level that the men at my job seemed to achieve so quickly. Like you, even though I knew that things needed to change, I didn't know where to start, and I was too overwhelmed to take on anything new anyway.

After years of frustrating trial and error, moments of self-doubt, and even humiliation, I figured out how to make an impact at work and command respect while ensuring that I have time for the things that matter most to me. Like helping with homework and taking family trips around the world. Like lecturing on innovation at universities and doing pro bono strategy consulting for local nonprofits.

For the past ten years, I have been sought out as a mentor and coach for midcareer professionals. In 2018, I launched the Lady Visitor Project, an online resource to collect and share wisdom from women who are excelling in male-dominated industries. To date, the project has insights from over eighty women across a broad range of industries over four continents.

Based on my own experience and the insights I have collected from the Lady Visitor Project, I will teach you:

1. How to assess if you are truly good enough to reach your goals.
2. How to claim your voice and command respect, with scripts for important conversations, meetings, and interviews.
3. How to develop a career roadmap that YOU control.
4. How to take on new challenges at work and still have time for yourself and your family.
5. How to handle the haters, and what to do when your colleagues, friends, and family decide that you are too ambitious.

Would you rather just keep doing what you are doing? Maybe you hope one day your boss and colleagues will finally acknowledge your talent. Maybe one day all those productivity hacks will actually work, and you will find more time for the people and projects you love. Maybe one day you won't ever feel guilty for missing a deadline or a family event.

But if you are tired of waiting for that one day to arrive, do something different. If you don't want to be left behind, judged, or undervalued, act now.

But be forewarned. If you want hacks and quick tips, you won't find them here. Navigating these challenges is going to take work. Similarly, if you want sob stories and outrage about how the system is rigged against us, you won't find those here, either. You already know that women like us face obstacles in our chosen path. And you have decided to keep going anyway.

The focus of this book is to help you get to your dream career faster and with less frustration. It will give you what most corporate HR programs, well-intentioned mentors, and general books about women at work can't: a proven roadmap for women just like you to get your ideas heard and make a significant impact in the field you love, all so you can have the career of your dreams and still have time for the things you care about the most.

THE FIRST KEY:

HOW TO TELL IF YOU'RE GOOD ENOUGH TO REACH YOUR GOALS

CHAPTER 1

WHY SMART, TALENTED TRAILBLAZERS FEEL UNDERESTIMATED AND SIDELINED

"I wish my male colleagues knew how often I am not called 'Dr.' and how often I am mistaken for an assistant instead of a faculty member; how students are harder on me than my male co-instructors and how I will get comments on my appearance. How I have to walk into every classroom dressed better and more prepared than them."

—ANGELA

In this chapter, you will learn:
1.   How our workplaces fill us with self-doubt.
2.   How to assess if your career goals are realistic.
3.   How to block out messages of self-doubt.

HOW OUR WORKPLACES FILL US WITH SELF-DOUBT

Early on in my university studies, I got the message that I wasn't good enough to reach my goals. It was always a dream of mine to get my PhD. When I told my chemical engineering professors, they laughed at me (literally, in my face—I will never forget it). The feedback was clear: "You are not good enough" to be one of us.

Fortunately, I had other people on my side. When I told my calculus teacher what happened, she suggested I speak with her husband about my desire to pursue research. It turned out that her husband, Dr. Harold Schobert, was the director of one of the most prestigious research institutes on campus. I walked into his office and told him I was interested in research and asked if he would consider taking me on as an intern. He said, "Sure, here is a project." Originally, I was planning to join the Air Force and hopefully go back to school someday. Instead, I got my PhD right away with Harold as my advisor.

But it wasn't easy. During my coursework, classmates— especially male classmates—lamented how getting a job was going to be so much easier for me when I was finished. "Recruiters are going to love you—a Black woman," my officemate said on a regular basis. As a result, when I was profiled in the now-defunct publication *Graduating Engineer & Computer Careers*, I said, "I do feel a sensitivity to the notion that I am where I am only because I am an African American woman. People have actually articulated that to me directly and others have insinuated it, so sometimes I've felt a bit like I have had to wear my resume on my chest."

It has been twenty years since that interview, yet sometimes I still feel that way. And I am not alone.[1] A poll of the eighty women in my Lady Visitor Project LinkedIn group shows that 68 percent of them have felt that their colleagues questioned their credentials.

Figure 1. Survey: Do My Colleagues Think I Am a Diversity Hire?

At some point in my career I felt that my colleagues thought I was a "diversity hire".
You can see how people vote. **Learn more**

Yes ⊘	68%
No	32%

Women like us can consistently get the subtle message at work that we didn't really earn our place. It can be the well-intentioned HR manager who says, "Let's add Julia to the program; we need more women." Or the female VP who says, "We are going to have to lay off some people, but don't worry—they are not going to get rid of us because we are diversity."

Other times, the messages are more overt. Like in my case when, during a performance review, my boss agreed that I had exceeded all my objectives. In his closing comments, he then chose to tell me, "I have decided that it's better if I give presentations to the leadership team instead of you because I am more attractive than you are." I really couldn't tell if he was joking. In hindsight, it's clear this was an inappropriate comment. But at that moment, it was devastating. My only thought was that my boss thought so little of me that he would use his power to keep me from progressing in my career. And on what basis? Not my merits, since he had clearly said I was an overperformer. But because of my looks.

All of these messages can make us doubt how we got to where we are and if we deserve to go further.

We get the same kind of suggestions outside of work. I analyzed recent news headlines of women who have achieved big promotions. Many times, the press release focuses only on the fact that she is a woman. There is no mention of her qualifications, or even her name! Whereas when men are promoted to leadership roles, their names are always in the headline, immediately followed by their previous roles.

Figure 2. Women in the Headlines

HEADLINE	NAME IN HEADLINE?	QUALIFICATIONS HIGHLIGHTED IN THE FIRST 3 LINES?	HEADLINE GRADE
Another Crack in the Glass Ceiling: Citigroup's Next CEO Is a Woman (NPR)	No (Jane Fraser)	No (President of Citi and the chief executive officer of global consumer banking)	F
Daughter of Immigrants Sworn in as 1st Black Woman on NJ Supreme Court (ABC)	No (Fabiana Pierre-Louis)	No (Assistant United States attorney in the office of United States Attorney for the District of New Jersey)	F
Amid 22% Jump in Sales, Clorox Names Female CEO (Forbes)	No (Linda Rendle)	Yes	C
Amazon Names First Black Executive to Bezos's Ruling Council (Bloomberg)	No (Alicia Boler Davis)	Yes	C
Imperva Appoints Pam Murphy as CEO (Information Age)	Yes	Yes	A

HEADLINE	NAME IN HEADLINE?	QUALIFICATIONS HIGHLIGHTED IN THE FIRST 3 LINES?	HEADLINE GRADE
MALE EXAMPLES			
Thierry Bolloré Appointed as the New Chief Executive Officer of Jaguar Land Rover (Economic Times) *An exemplar for men. The headlines all look like this!*	Yes	Yes	A
Reddit Names Y Combinator CEO Michael Seibel as Alexis Ohanian's Replacement (The Verge)	Yes	Yes	A+ *(They get a bonus point for not putting "Black man" in the title given that there is a picture accompanying the article and I can see!)*

HOW TO ASSESS IF YOUR CAREER GOALS ARE REALISTIC

But then I had a watershed moment.

Three months into the job at my new firm, I was invited to present my first impressions to the leadership team.

When I walked into the room, I was greeted with smiles and handshakes. Since I was participating for a short session in the afternoon, I had to find a place to sit among the scattered coats, and briefcases in the room. My new boss walked over to a laptop and gently tossed it down on the table, effectively displacing someone who had been sitting there. "Here," he said, "I want you to sit right next to me". I did, and I gave my presentation to an audience of executives who were generally interested in my insights.

For several days afterward, I reflected on my two very different experiences with presenting to the leadership of my firm. In the first case, I was excluded from even entering the room. In the second case, I was welcomed.

What was the difference between the Angelique who wasn't good enough to be in the same room with the leaders of the company she'd worked at for twenty years and the Angelique who was the featured speaker with leaders in her new firm?

Not one single thing.

No, really. The external factors were different—the context, the decision makers, the objectives, etc. But I was the same.

Maybe, I had always been good enough.

Here is how you can test whether you are good enough.

EXERCISE 1: REALISTIC GOALS ASSESSMENT

Read the following list and circle any statements that are true for you.

1. I have been accused of only being a diversity hire.

2. I have been mistaken for the secretary or a teaching assistant.

3. I have had my ideas stolen in a meeting.

4. I have been excluded from after-work social activities because, "it's just the guys watching sports."

5. I have wasted my time at work social activities so I could be perceived as "one of the guys."

6. I have had to leave a meeting and walk to another building to find a bathroom.

7. I have been told I am too ambitious.

8. I have been told I am too direct, or not direct enough.

9. I have been told not to be so hard on a peer because it will hurt his ego.

10. I have been told to smile no matter how I actually feel.

Did you circle any of the questions?

Yes?

You passed! You are good enough.

How do I know?

Because you have already figured out how to get to where you are today despite having to go through the adversities I listed above, as well as probably much, much more.

Let me repeat this just in case you missed it. You have already demonstrated that you are smart, tenacious, thoughtful, and resilient. You have already persevered through rigorous training in what was likely a challenging and sometimes isolating environment. You already have what it takes to do anything you want. Don't get me wrong, you might have skills or experience gaps, and I will teach you how to identify them in Chapter 5. But you are most definitely good enough.

Not convinced?

Of course, you're not. Women in male-dominated fields like STEM are three times more likely to feel like they have to provide more evidence of their competence than others do.[2]

But here is the problem. If you don't think you are good enough, nobody else will, either. The very first step to convincing your future employer that you are good enough to take on that new role is to convince yourself first. But with so many cues around you suggesting that you aren't good enough, how do you change your mind?

HOW TO BLOCK OUT MESSAGES OF SELF-DOUBT

If you are like me, you often have your head down getting the work done, and you don't take the time to celebrate all of the great things you have accomplished. As a result, self-doubt can creep into your mind and take hold. You can stop that process from happening by filling your mind with the truth. The truth is you have already accomplished a lot in your career. You just need to acknowledge it.

Celebrate big wins

The Accomplishments Inventory is a list of all the great things you have done. The purpose of this exercise is two-fold. First, it's going to help you realize and remember how competent and capable you already are. Second, it will serve as the basis for developing your professional profile, a document that you will need later to help you achieve your next career goal.

EXERCISE 2: ACCOMPLISHMENTS INVENTORY

You will need your free *You are More than a Diversity Hire®: Women in STEM Workbook* or two sheets of paper. On the first sheet, label it "Brainstorm." On the second sheet, make four columns with the titles "Description," "Internal Relevance," "Success Metric," and "External Relevance." It should look like this:

Figure 3. Accomplishments Inventory Template

DESCRIPTION Describe what happened and how. "I achieved _____ by doing _____."	INTERNAL RELEVANCE Why is the accomplishment important to me?	SUCCESS METRIC How is the accomplishment quantified?	EXTERNAL RELEVANCE Why is the accomplishment important to your organization or to someone else?

STEP 1: BRAINSTORM.

Try to set aside one hour of uninterrupted time. Start by just brainstorming all your accomplishments and writing them down.

Here are a few prompts to help you get started:

- What are you proud of?
- What were some "firsts" for you?
- When were you an "only"? The only woman in your class, the only woman on the team, the only?
- When did you overachieve a goal?
- When did you partially achieve a goal under adverse conditions?

STEP 2: DESCRIBE YOUR ACCOMPLISHMENTS.

Take each item from your list and start it as a new row under accomplishments. To describe your accomplishments in a consistent way that will work for you in later exercises, try to write them in the following format:

"I achieved *accomplishment* by doing *action(s)*."

Don't spend more than one to two minutes trying to format each accomplishment. You can always come back to it later.

STEP 3: INTERNAL RELEVANCE. WHY IS THIS ACCOMPLISHMENT IMPORTANT TO YOU?

- Why did you write this accomplishment down?
- Does it meet a career objective?
- Does it meet a personal goal?
- Does it make you smile when you think about it?

STEP 4: DEFINE THE SUCCESS METRICS.

For each accomplishment, think about how you or others can quantify the impact of the accomplishment.

Common metrics include:

- Money (i.e., $, €)
- Time (weeks, minutes, seconds)
- Frequency (times per week, times per month)

STEP 5: EXTERNAL RELEVANCE. WHY IS THIS ACCOMPLISHMENT IMPORTANT TO OTHERS?

Put yourself in the place of the recipient of your efforts. Even if you weren't thanked, or if the actions weren't received in the way you intended, what were you trying to accomplish?

Here is an example of how to use the inventory.

Figure 4. Accomplishments Inventory Example

DESCRIPTION Describe what happened and how. "I achieved _____ by doing _____."	INTERNAL RELEVANCE Why is the accomplishment important to me?	SUCCESS METRIC How is the accomplishment quantified?	EXTERNAL RELEVANCE Why is the accomplishment important to your organization or to someone else?
I earned $12M in new revenue by launching a technology licensing initiative.	I worked really hard on this project and overcame several obstacles, including beating out a far bigger competitor.	Revenue ($M)	By delivering this new client, the team exceeded their objectives for the year. This helped the business and brought credibility to the team.

STEP 6. REVIEW AND UPDATE.

Review this list every week. Make updates as needed.

Soon, you should have a nice list of accomplishments. Congratulations! I hope you are now convinced that with this track record of achievements, you can take things to the next level in your career.

Don't stop there. It's a trap to only count "big" accomplishments. You can end up thinking that you don't do anything "worth noting" very often. There are other things that you do on a regular basis that you should notice and reflect on.

Celebrate small wins

According to Harvard researcher Teresa Amabile,[3] of all the things that can boost emotions, motivation, and perceptions during a workday, the single most important thing is making progress in meaningful work. And the more frequently people experience that sense of progress—even a small win—can make all the difference in how they feel and perform. She and co-author Steven Kramer go on to say that the act of writing it down releases mood-enhancing chemicals in our brains.

I vividly remember the mood-boosting effects of a small win when I interviewed for the executive MBA program at MIT. On my way to the interview, I was stopped by a young African American man collecting money for a charity. Since I had time before I needed to be at the interview, I let him make his pitch. I donated and casually asked him how he had come to be doing this work. He mentioned that he was studying engineering. He was considering graduate school but had doubts about whether he was good enough. He was doing this charity work to take some time off and gain perspective.

I told him that I had a PhD in STEM and a little more about what I did for a living. I gave him a lot of encouragement to try graduate school, and I gave him my card and told him that if he wanted to talk more, he could call me anytime. He started to tear up. He said I was the nicest person he had met since he started, and he asked if he could give me a hug.

For me, that was a small win. In the five minutes that we were talking on the sidewalk, I had lifted someone up—and that had lifted me up. I felt good and had a huge smile on my face as I walked across the street to the interview. So I was undeterred when the interview location didn't match what was on my invitation, even though I was certain about where it was supposed to be, having confirmed the location and walked the route the night before. Politely and cheerfully, I asked the staff to help me find the place where I needed to be. I was not nervous when I had to wait with other candidates, my competition. I was happy to chat them up. That brief hug from that young man erased my interview jitters.

My credentials got me into the program, but my demeanor was notable to them. How do I know? They told me. As a side note, the MIT Executive MBA team is a bit secretive about their interview process. I have reason to believe that they created that little location mix-up on purpose just to see what we would do. Believe me, not everyone was gracious about having to find the new place.

Another example of a personal small win was a text I got out of the blue from my mom. I am always thrilled to get a note that my kids are behaving well and displaying the values we are trying to teach them.

> **Seth and Sophia were very kind to a special needs teenager and his 3 year old brother at the park. You would be very proud of them.** 👍🖤

Only you can decide what is considered a big win and what is small. It's purely a judgment call. One way to think about it is if you would put it on your resume, it's a big win. If you feel good about it but you wouldn't put it on your resume, it's a small win. Here is a short list of things to consider:[4]

1. Receiving Praise
2. Meeting Thirty-Day Goals
3. Speaking Up
4. Being Asked for Advice
5. Receiving Gratitude
6. Demonstrating EQ
7. Hacking Productivity
8. Being Assertive
9. Presenting to Others
10. Tackling a Tough Task
11. Feeling Energized
12. Helping Others

EXERCISE 3: SMALL WINS INVENTORY

You will need your workbook or two sheets of paper. On the first sheet, label it "Brainstorm." On the second sheet, make two columns with the headings "Small Win" and "Internal Relevance." It should look like this:

Figure 5. Small Wins Inventory Template

DESCRIPTION Describe what happened and how.	INTERNAL RELEVANCE Why is the accomplishment important to me?

STEP 1. REVIEW YOUR LIST OF ACCOMPLISHMENTS FROM THE PREVIOUS BRAINSTORM.

Go back to your list of accomplishments. Anything that you didn't think was big or important enough to list as an accomplishment? Maybe you struggled to figure out the right metrics or why it was important. That is okay. Put it on this list of small wins.

STEP 2. BRAINSTORM AGAIN.

- When did you get a pat on the back from a friend or colleague?
- When did you wish you had gotten a pat on the back from a friend or colleague?

- When did you make someone else smile?
- When did you teach someone something new?

STEP 3. DESCRIBE EACH ITEM ON THE LIST.

STEP 4. INTERNAL RELEVANCE. WHY IS THIS ACCOMPLISHMENT IMPORTANT TO YOU?

- Why did you write this accomplishment down?
- Does it make you smile when you think about it?

Here is an example of one of my recent small wins.

Figure 6. Small Wins Inventory Example

DESCRIPTION Describe what happened and how.	INTERNAL RELEVANCE Why is the accomplishment important to me?
I received a surprise thank-you letter in the mail from a neighbor for engaging her elderly mother in a conversation during the weekend barbecue. She was grateful that I had treated her mother like a whole person and made no assumption that she wouldn't have anything to contribute because of her age. It's sad that my neighbor feels like her mother is ignored.	Being kind is one of my core values. It was a nice acknowledgement that I had done that without really trying.

DESCRIPTION Describe what happened and how.	INTERNAL RELEVANCE Why is the accomplishment important to me?
I received a text from a former employee saying he used one of the communication tools that I had taught him, and it really helped him in his new role.	Giving back is an important value of mine. It's nice to know that something I did helped someone else.

STEP 5: REVIEW AND UPDATE.

What I want you to do is build the habit of reflecting and acknowledging that you are doing positive and impactful things in your daily life and in your career. Review your Small Wins Inventory every day and update it.

RECAP

You have been getting subtle and strong messages that you are not good enough for a long time. Those messages are wrong. You have the proof right in front of you. You have already overcome adversity and made important contributions to your job. No matter where you are in your career, you have more to give. Block out the negative messages by reminding yourself every week and every day.

THE SECOND KEY:

HOW TO COMMAND
RESPECT AT WORK

CHAPTER 2

TO COMMAND RESPECT, YOU MUST REMAIN CALM

"I am an interrupter,
it's the only way I can get heard."

—ANDREA

In this chapter, you will learn:

1. The two must-haves for commanding respect at work.
2. How to determine what is keeping you from being cool, calm, and collected.
3. How to manage heated emotions at work.

THE TWO MUST-HAVES FOR COMMANDING RESPECT AT WORK

"I don't take orders from you, missy," was written on Post-it Notes scattered around the lab. In my first job, I worked with a technician who refused to take my direction. He didn't like the idea of a twenty-five-year-old woman telling him, a fifty-seven-year-old man, what to do. When I tried to explain to my boss what was going on, I faltered. And his condescending response was so maddening that I ended up shedding a few tears. I had become a crier. He mistook my tears to mean that my feelings were hurt rather than what they actually were—a result of me trying to contain my rage. Hence, he took pity on me and suggested that we all "hug it out."

I was sure that having my boss's pity was not commanding respect. I never shed a tear in the office again.

As a result, I kept everything bottled up. But holding in emotions all the time is hard. It led to me becoming what I like to call an "erupter." Whenever I tried to convey my point and felt that my colleagues weren't listening, I would hold it in until I couldn't take it anymore, and I would roll my eyes or huff or engage in some other spontaneous reaction to display my frustration. That behavior led to a colleague writing in my "anonymous" performance feedback: "Angelique needs to stop acting like a petulant child."

I was sure that being called a "petulant child" was also not commanding respect.

I was missing two key ingredients to commanding respect:

1. A way to be calm enough to say what I wanted to say without crying or rolling my eyes.
2. Confidence to claim my voice so people would listen to me.

HOW TO FIGURE OUT WHAT IS KEEPING YOU FROM BEING COOL, CALM, AND COLLECTED

Handling negative emotions in the workplace is a challenge for everyone. Women, in particular, are expected to smile and be friendly all of the time. If we express anger or frustration, we are seen as being emotional, irrational, or disrespectful.[5] But there are people in your organization who are a**holes. Sometimes just to you, sometimes to everyone.[6] And there are others who drive you crazy for specific reasons.

So what are you supposed to do?

First, realize that your feelings are completely normal.[7] Second, realize that not having a way to manage your emotions and your reactions is hurting your ability to command respect on the job.[8, 9] The way to solve this problem is to build up your emotional intelligence.[10]

According to *Psychology Today*, emotional intelligence is the ability to identify and manage one's own emotions, as well as the emotions of others.[11] Emotional intelligence is a very broad and popular topic in both business and academic literature.[12, 13, 14] A full treatment is beyond the scope of this book. Below is a graphic summarizing the twelve components of emotional intelligence. I am going to focus on proven strategies to help you with the first two elements: emotional self-awareness and emotional self-control. I have found that having the tools to address these two elements has made a significant impact on my ability to remain cool, calm, and collected at work.

Figure 7. The Twelve Elements of Emotional Intelligence[15]

SELF-AWARENESS	SELF-MANAGEMENT	SOCIAL AWARENESS	RELATIONSHIP MANAGEMENT
Emotional Self-Awareness	Emotional Self-Control	Empathy	Influence
	Adaptability		Coach and Mentor
	Achievement Orientation	Organizational Awareness	Conflict Management
	Positive Outlook		Teamwork
			Inspirational Leadership

How others impact you

Self-awareness is the ability to recognize and understand your moods and emotions and how they impact others. The first step is to understand what you are feeling and why. I have had the most success with improving my self-awareness by proactively doing observation and self-reflection through the Enjoy/Dread List.[16] The purpose of this exercise is to establish a list of the kinds of people you enjoy being around and the kind of people you dread being around. In doing this exercise, you can come to understand the words and behaviors that others use that cause you to react in a way that undermines your ability to stay calm and confident at work.

Here is how to do it.

EXERCISE 4: ENJOY/DREAD LIST

You will need your workbook or two sheets of paper. Label the first page "Brainstorm." On the second page, make two columns. The first column is labeled "I enjoy being around people who" and the second column is labeled "I dread being around people who." It should look like this:

Figure 8. Enjoy/Dread List Template

I *ENJOY* BEING AROUND PEOPLE WHO:	I *DREAD* BEING AROUND PEOPLE WHO:

STEP 1: BRAINSTORM

Take ten minutes and reflect on these questions. If anything comes to mind, please note it on your sheet.

- Who do you enjoy working with? What behaviors or words do they use to make you feel that way?
- For the "enjoy" side of your list, go back to your Small Wins Inventory. Did you collaborate with anyone to achieve these wins? Was it a good experience, and why?
- For the "dread" side of your list, think about who bothers you at work. What behaviors or words do they use to make you feel that way?

STEP 2: ANALYZE AND SYNTHESIZE

Take a look at your brainstorm list. Do you see any patterns?

Based on your analysis, fill in the Enjoy/Dread List.

This will be round one.

STEP 3: NOTICE AND NAME

Now it's time to dig deeper. For the next two weeks, try to notice when you are feeling really energized by your interactions with people and when you are either completely drained or frustrated. Name what is going on in those situations. Who was there, where were you, and what were you talking about? Do the same analysis that you did for round one, and add the information to your list.

Here is what my list looks like:

Figure 9. Enjoy/Dread List Example

I *ENJOY* BEING AROUND PEOPLE WHO:	I *DREAD* BEING AROUND PEOPLE WHO:
Are coachable	Think they know everything
Are optimistic	Are pessimistic
Are trustworthy	Use words and actions that don't match
Seek to find how they can improve	Are complainers
Don't blame others	Blame others for their situations

I *ENJOY* BEING AROUND PEOPLE WHO:	I *DREAD* BEING AROUND PEOPLE WHO:
Are kind to other people, to marginalized groups, and to animals	Are disrespectful, insult people, and interrupt
Want a process	Want a quick fix
Are respectful of my time and efforts	Are late
Acknowledge the help and support of others	Are braggarts
Are problem solvers	Are only out for the money
Are solution oriented	Don't follow through on their commitments

I had a problem with an engineer on my team. I started to avoid him because every time I talked to him, I would leave the conversation annoyed and frustrated. For almost any request for a new assignment or a change to an existing one, he launched into a brief but passionate soliloquy about how the plan wasn't perfect. He didn't have a suggestion on how to make it better; he just had opinions on why it wasn't perfect. I talked to him directly about his behavior, but he didn't seem willing or capable of changing. On the other hand, he always did what was asked of him, on time and with outstanding quality. So I had a dilemma.

Then I did the Enjoy/Dread List exercise. I realized that he was a complainer. That explained why I was always so frustrated. Why complainers annoy me isn't important. The important part was that once I framed my interactions with him as me listening to a complainer, I understood the reason why I was so frustrated. I also discovered something else when I paid attention to my interactions with him. He always started his complaint with the phrase "It is a pity that ...." After doing this exercise, whenever I heard that phrase, I took a deep breath. When he finished with his complaint, I would say, "Yes, it is a pity." Then I moved on to the task at hand. It was a win-win. I got through the discussions with ease, and he was happy that I increased my interactions with him.

How you impact others

The second aspect of self-awareness is understanding how your behavior impacts others. The only real way to do this is to get frequent, honest, constructive feedback from your colleagues.[17] Feedback is very important, and as you continue to progress in your career, you will need to find ways to get it. This is difficult to do. Women get less constructive feedback at work.18, [19] Also, if you already think your colleagues don't respect you, you might be skeptical of the feedback you get. The most important aspect of feedback is to check in with yourself to see if you agree.

I was fortunate to work with an executive coach, Cory, during my time at MIT. During our first session, we were to go over a lengthy summary of the feedback I had gotten from my colleagues during a 360-degree assessment. I was nervous to go over the assessment because, among the many stellar comments about how great I was, I had also received the comment I'd mentioned earlier in this chapter: "Angelique needs to stop acting like a petulant child." I was certain that Cory was going to want to talk about that in detail.

Instead, I was shocked that she didn't mention it. She asked me what I wanted to work on. I mentioned the "petulant child" comment, and she asked, "Do you think you act like a petulant child?" I said, "No." And that was it. The idea that I didn't have to accept the comment as fact just because someone had said it about me was a revelation.

HOW TO MANAGE HEATED EMOTIONS AT WORK

Now that you have some ideas about the kinds of people or situations that cause you to react negatively, you need to figure out what to do about it. Emotional self-control is the ability to keep your disruptive emotions and impulses in check and to maintain your effectiveness under stressful or even hostile conditions.[20]

Before I get into how to build up your self-control skills, I want to make sure you understand what self-control is not. It's not bottling things up. It's not accepting unacceptable behavior. Rather, self-control means noticing the feelings and their accompanying bodily signals, and choosing whether or how to act on them.[21] The power is in giving yourself enough space to make a choice.

A good example of creating this space was when I had to deal with a disastrous presentation to a project sponsor. My team and I had worked on the project for four months, and this was the final report out that showed our conclusions and results. The project sponsor was not happy. It was like he had forgotten what we had initially been assigned to do because he immediately stopped the presentation and told me that we had answered the wrong question. Then he proceeded to criticize all parts of our analysis. Four months of work went up in flames in ninety seconds. We captured the feedback and closed the meeting. I was furious. Specifically, I was furious at my boss who had given me the assignment, determined the scope and deliverables, and provided feedback for the two rounds of dry runs we had done before the final presentation. I felt like he had really set us up for failure. And furthermore, during the meeting, he had failed to step up and take any accountability for his part in the assignment.

I wrote him a scathing message, telling him that I thought he had failed us. Then, I didn't send it. At that moment, I knew I was angry and disappointed and that I shouldn't be communicating these feelings to my boss in a chat. I made the choice to erase it. The following day, I scheduled a meeting with him to debrief, and it was during that time that I told him how I felt. I was much calmer and had thought through my points. He agreed that he had left us out to dry and apologized. He also gave me constructive feedback on the presentation and some insights into recent events elsewhere in the firm that might have contributed to the project sponsor's reaction to our presentation. Overall, it was a very productive conversation.

That is what we want. We want to be able to make the choice. In this case, I chose to address what I thought was unfair behavior—but only when I was calmer.

How can you create the space to make a choice?

If you are like me, you might find that by going through the Enjoy/Dread List exercise, you have given yourself a head start. Now that you know in advance the specific people, behaviors, or words that cause you to react, you can be better in tune with yourself. You can be prepared, take a deep breath, and power through.

Other times, this might not be enough, and you will need specific tools to get you through the interaction.

I think of these self-control tools on two levels:

1. Tools that help you to diffuse your frustration **in the moment** in a specific situation.
2. Tools that help you lower your baseline stress level and remain calm **all the time**.

Remaining calm in the moment

Before my first trip to Saudi Arabia, I had a meeting with a cultural advisor, Samira, to explain to me the very different cultural norms in Saudi Arabia versus the United States. As we walked through my journey from getting on the plane, traveling through customs, going to the hotel, and getting to my meetings, she explained several likely scenarios.

- You might be separated from your male colleagues during customs and immigration. But you will be perfectly safe. Remain calm.
- You may find that people stare at you, even though you will be dressed appropriately. It will be obvious to them that you are a foreign woman, which is rare. Remain calm.
- You may find that people don't make eye contact with you at all. Remain calm.
- You may find that men leave the elevator if you try to enter. Remain calm.

I had the refrain in my mind throughout my travels. But then something she didn't mention happened. It was time for my big presentation, and as I walked up to the podium, half of the audience stood up and walked out of the room, just because I was a woman. My male colleagues who had come on the trip with me were all looking down and fiddling with their pens because they were so embarrassed for me. The men in the audience who stayed were staring at me, wondering what I was going to do next.

Despite the wave of humiliation that passed over me, I remembered Samira's advice: Remain calm. I managed to hold back the tears, plaster a smile on my face, and say, "I am so glad to be here with you today," before launching into my presentation. I saved my tears for later that night when I called my husband. Don't worry, the story has a happy ending. My team earned a multimillion-dollar contract with the group from Saudi Arabia. By the time I left the company, the team leader was asking to talk to me on a monthly basis and, later on, used me as a reference to get a visa.

Based on my own experience, I recommend two techniques for managing stress in the moment:

1.   Taking a deep breath.
2.   Reciting a calming phrase in your mind.

In addition to the techniques that work for me, expert recommendations include: progressive relaxation[22] and the five-finger relaxation technique.[23]

EXERCISE 5: ONE-WEEK SELF-CONTROL TECHNIQUE PRACTICE

You will need your workbook or one sheet of paper. On the top of your paper, write, "One-Week Self-Control Technique Practice." Create a table with four columns and eight rows. Label the columns "Day," "AM," "Afternoon," and "PM." It should look like this:

Figure 10. One-Week Self-Control Technique Template

SELF-CONTROL TECHNIQUES

Pick one you like and try it every day for seven days.

- Deep breathing
- Reciting a calming phrase
- Progressive relaxation
- Five-finger relaxation technique

Write down what you notice after trying each self-control technique.

DAY	AM	AFTERNOON	PM
1			
2			
3			
4			
5			
6			
7			

STEP 1: SELECT A SELF-CONTROL TECHNIQUE TO TRY.

I have listed a few here, but if you want to try something different, please do.

- Deep breathing
- Reciting a calming phrase
- Progressive relaxation
- Five-finger relaxation technique

STEP 2: FIND TIME DURING THE DAY TO TRY YOUR SELF-CONTROL TECHNIQUE THREE TIMES.

STEP 3: AT THE DESIGNATED TIME, TRY YOUR SELF-CONTROL TECHNIQUE.

STEP 4: WRITE DOWN HOW YOU FEEL.

How did doing the self-control technique make you feel?

STEP 5: TRY THE TECHNIQUE FOR A WEEK.

If you feel more relaxed than you did before you started the week, continue to practice your self-control technique once a day for the next week. If you don't feel relaxed, try a different technique.

Your goal is to find something that makes you feel more relaxed and to practice it regularly so that whenever a stressful situation arises, you have a strategy ready to use.

Remaining Calm All The Time

Full disclosure: I am not good at this. I have borderline hypertension and occasional bouts of insomnia. I have tried a bunch of things, and I am still experimenting. First, I will tell you what the experts say. Then, I am going to tell you what seems to be working for me now.

There are tens of thousands of books about stress reduction. They all basically say the same thing. Too much stress has a negative impact on the body.[24] Here are commonly accepted ways to reduce it:[25]

1. Nutritious diet
2. Regular amounts of moderate exercise
3. Six to eight hours of quality sleep
4. Mindfulness
5. Meditation

I have also had experience with lesser-known strategies. I learned about hypnosis when I was pregnant with my first child. I was so riddled with anxiety about the health of the pregnancy that I had insomnia. And when I was able to fall asleep, I had nightmares. My doctor said it was "normal," but I didn't feel normal. So I did some research and found an audio program called Hypbirth. I started to listen to the first track, and what happened next was strange. I didn't remember anything about it. I tried it two more times. I would fall asleep almost immediately when the track started and wake up when the voice said, "And now you will awaken feeling positive and relaxed."

After three days, I was sleeping without nightmares. The results were so startling that I asked my husband to watch me the next time I listened to the program, just to make sure nothing weird was happening. He told me, "It just looks like you're sleeping." Since then, I have been hooked. I have been listening to hypnosis/guided meditations ever since. I use the audio programs when I am having trouble falling asleep or have a specific issue that is causing me anxiety.[26]

Another tool that helps me reduce stress is the Pomodoro Technique.[27] The Pomodoro Technique is a productivity technique, not a stress-reduction technique. But I have found it really helps me reduce stress because it combats procrastination-induced anxiety. When I procrastinate enough, I start to have anxiety about not meeting deadlines.

The basic idea is deceptively simple.[28] You just set a timer for twenty-five minutes, and focus on the task at hand. When the timer goes off, set it for five minutes and take a break. Repeat. Take a longer break after a few rounds. There are many books on the subject, and there are ways to optimize the approach in terms of how to select the things to do in each twenty-five minute block. For me, just setting the timer is enough to get me back on track. I feel better when I have accomplished something toward my goal, and my stress level goes down.

Try some different stress-reduction techniques and see what works for you.

EXERCISE 6. THIRTY-DAY STRESS-REDUCTION CHALLENGE

You will need your workbook or one sheet of paper. At the top of your paper, write: "The Thirty-Day Stress-Reduction Challenge." At the very bottom of your paper, write: "Stress-Reduction Goal." In the middle, create a table with five rows and six columns so you have thirty spaces. It will look like this:

Figure 11. Thirty-Day Stress-Reduction Challenge Template

My stress reduction goal: _____.

1 Yay, you started!	2	3	4	5
6	7	8	9	10
11	12	13	14	15 Halfway there.
16	17	18	19	20
21	22	23	24	25
26	27	28	29	30 Done!

STEP 1: SELECT A RELAXATION TECHNIQUE.

I have suggested a few, but you can pick whatever you want.

STEP 2: SELECT A GOAL.

What do you hope to accomplish by being more relaxed?

- Do you want to sleep better?
- Do you want to be calmer at work?
- Do you want to reduce your blood pressure?
- Whatever goal you select, write it down at the bottom of your sheet.

STEP 3. SCHEDULE TIME.

On your calendar, put the necessary time you need to complete the stress-reduction technique that you chose.

STEP 4: TRACK YOUR PROGRESS.

Tick off your daily accomplishments.

STEP 5: ANALYZE YOUR RESULTS.

- Did achieve your goal or get closer to it?
- Did you notice anything else that happened when you tried this?
- Do you want to keep going to try something else?

RECAP

In order to command respect, you must be calm. Workplaces are fraught with forces that make that difficult. There are people who will push your buttons and make it hard for you to calmly state your ideas. There are high-stakes situations that cause you anxiety. But you can handle both scenarios by being prepared. Be prepared to have a reaction when that person says something annoying or hurtful by understanding yourself better. Notice and name the feeling and have a strategy to cope. Implement at least one stress-reduction technique to help yourself be calmer all the time.

CHAPTER 3:

TO COMMAND RESPECT, YOU MUST CLAIM YOUR VOICE IN TRICKY SITUATIONS

"When I speak up at work, I am called bitchy or whiny. When I don't speak up, I get dinged for not contributing. I get so many mixed messages I don't know how to behave."

—KIM

In this chapter, you will learn:
1. How to promote your own accomplishments.
2. How to stand out in high-stakes meetings.
3. How to handle interrupters and idea stealers.

There is a lot of information out there about the differences in communication between men and women and how women's natural communication style can put them at a disadvantage in the workplace.[29, 30] As someone who works almost entirely with men, I can tell you that there are a lot of men who are perceived as poor communicators. They can use too many words. They can use the wrong words for the audience or meander off on tangents. They can use filler words, upspeak, and other verbal distractions. In the end, both men and women can fail to effectively get their point across.

Therefore, I am not going to focus on perceived communication deficiencies that women might have in the workplace because I don't think we have any specific to us. Rather, I am going to share recommendations I give everyone in my team on how to effectively communicate in common workplace situations. There are three situations that I think are especially important to get proficient at: promoting your accomplishments, getting noticed in high-stakes meetings, and managing interrupters and idea stealers. I will give you strategies for each one.

TRICKY SITUATION #1: PROMOTING YOUR OWN ACCOMPLISHMENTS

The first communication scenario that is fraught with pitfalls, but important to master, is bragging about yourself. Your colleagues will respect you more if they have a better appreciation for what you have done and what you can do. You absolutely must promote yourself to peers and managers within your organization and in your personal network. And you can do it in a way that doesn't make you feel like a jerk.

We have all been there before. We are in a meeting, and Joe starts telling a story about how he did some great thing, and you think, *What a jerk; I never want to be like that.* But when it is your turn to actually state something relevant about how you have already successfully accomplished whatever it was that needed to be done, you either freeze or you don't feel confident about sharing your accomplishments to their full extent.

There are two problems. The first problem is with Joe. The reason that Joe seems like a jerk is because he probably framed his bragging in a long story or bragged about something that isn't relevant. So, you are forced to sit and listen, waiting in anticipation for the speaker to get to the point, only to learn that the point was that they were bragging about themselves. Maybe Joe is just always long-winded. Or maybe Joe was trying to use some flashy sales technique. In any case, it left you feeling annoyed.

The fact is you can state your relevant accomplishments in a concise way that avoids forcing your audience to wait in anticipation. If people want to know more about it, they will ask.

The second problem is with you and your own self-consciousness. Imagine this situation: a colleague asks you about your vacation, and you say, "We went to the beach. I found a great deal on a hotel by using our corporate perks."

Do you feel like a jerk? Is your heart racing? No?

Good, because you have just shared an accomplishment using the format we discussed in Exercise 1: Realistic Goals Assessment: "I accomplished *accomplishment* by doing *action(s)*." In this case, you accomplished *getting a good deal on the hotel* by *using the corporate perks*.

It was easy, right?

Now you will learn to do the same thing, but for accomplishments related to your career.

EXERCISE 7: BRAGGING THE RIGHT WAY

You will need your workbook or your summary from Exercise 2: The Accomplishments Inventory and one sheet of paper. Label the page "Self-Promotion Exercise" and make two columns. The first column is labeled "Accomplishment" and the second column is labeled "Feedback." It should look like this:

Figure 12. Bragging the Right Way Template

ACCOMPLISHMENT "I achieved _____ by doing _____ ."	FEEDBACK

STEP 1: SELECT A FEW RELEVANT ACCOMPLISHMENTS.

Go back to your accomplishments list and pick a few of them. Start to say them out loud, just to yourself first if you want.

STEP 2: PRACTICE IN A REAL CONVERSATION.

Think about the last few conversations you have had with colleagues. Can you think about the times when you wanted to mention an accomplishment but didn't? Use your accomplishment statements in a real conversation where it matters.

STEP 3: RECORD THE FEEDBACK YOU GET.

What is going to happen when you say this statement? A couple of things could happen:

1. Nothing.

2. The person you told will say, "Cool, tell me more about that."

When do you use this technique?

1. During meetings when you want to mention that you've accomplished something similar to what is being talked about.

2. In interviews, when an interviewer asks, "Tell me about a time when you . . ."

3. Random strangers (just kidding . . . or am I?).

I will talk more about how to use this technique again in Chapter 5: Figuring Out Your Next Career Move.

TRICKY SITUATION #2: STANDING OUT IN HIGH-STAKES MEETINGS

High-stakes meetings are meetings where you want to impress people. You know that this is a great opportunity to get your ideas heard and possibly dazzle leaders with your brilliance. The problem is when you get to the meeting, you choke! You are nervous that you are going to say the wrong thing and that people are going to think you are stupid. Or you are worried that you might inadvertently make a colleague look bad. You might have trouble following along in the meeting because they may be referring to terms, locations, or people that you aren't familiar with.

What started out as an exciting opportunity, morphs into you spending the meeting thinking, *What should I say, and when should I say it?* Eventually, about halfway through the meeting, you start saying to yourself, *Oh my god, I am going to miss this opportunity*, and now you are beating yourself up.

Sound familiar?

This happens to everyone. Before I give you the strategy, I need to give you some tough love: This idea that you are going to say the exact right thing at the exact right time in front of these important people is a fantasy. There are too many factors outside of your control to make that happen.

So just forget it.

But the good news is that there is still a way to be engaging and insightful, and that is by asking questions. I want you to change your mindset about what you want to accomplish in this meeting. Right now, you view the meeting as a place where you want to demonstrate your brilliance (in other words, a place where you have to perform). So things go wrong because you have performance anxiety. Instead, I want you to view the meeting as a place where you want to learn. And what you want to learn is the answer to your question. If you go into the meeting with a curiosity mindset instead of a performance mindset, you take the pressure off yourself, and you are more likely to speak.

What question should you ask?

I am definitely a firm believer in the fact that there are no stupid questions. However, some questions are better than others, especially in this context.

There are two go-to questions that are always on the mind of executives.

If you ask one of these questions, you will not only get your voice heard; you will also demonstrate that you are in tune with the concerns of high-level people.

Question 1: What are the benchmarks?

This an effective question because before an executive spends resources, she wants to know whether or not the initiative will work. And the way she gets confidence that it will work is by finding out if others have tried it in other departments in the firm or other companies outside of the firm.

Question 2: What are the metrics?

This is another good question because executives want to know how to measure whether or not their investment is successful. Ideally, the success factors can be boiled down to one or two things that can be put onto a scorecard so the executive doesn't have to think about it again until they see the report.

EXERCISE 8: HIGH-STAKES MEETING PREPARATION AND OUTCOME TRACKER

You will need your workbook or one sheet of paper. Label the page "Meeting Script and Success Tracker." It should look like this:

Figure 13. High-Stakes Meeting Preparation and Outcome Tracker Template

MEETING DESCRIPTION	YOUR OBJECTIVE	SCRIPT	OUTCOME
When and where is the meeting, who will be there, and what is the objective?	What do I want to learn?	1. What are the benchmarks? 2. What are the metrics? 3. Other customized question based on my analysis	What happened when I asked my question?

STEP 1: GET SOME BASIC INFO ABOUT THE MEETING.

To be the most effective in the meeting, you need to understand why the meeting is taking place and who will be there. Ideally, you would know in advance:

1. Who will be there.

2. Agenda.

3. Decision points if needed.

4. Why you were invited to the meeting.

It can actually be quite difficult to figure out what the meeting is actually about.[31] If it isn't obvious from the meeting notice or from input from other attendees, don't press too hard. People know that they "should" have agendas for meetings and can be sensitive if they perceive that they are being criticized.

If you are able to discern the basics of the meeting, you can determine in advance which of the two magic questions will work best in your situation. If you can't figure out the details, just prepare both questions.

STEP 2: REVIEW THE TWO QUESTIONS YOU COULD ASK DURING THE MEETING.

If you want to practice asking your questions, go ahead. Here is the delivery I recommend. Let's assume that the speaker's name is Jackson.

SCRIPT 1: HIGH STAKES MEETINGS, THE BENCHMARKS QUESTION

"Jackson, I have a question. What benchmarks were used to develop the approach for this initiative?" Write down Jackson's answer and say, "Thank you."

SCRIPT 2: HIGH STAKES MEETINGS, THE METRICS QUESTION

"Jackson, I have a question. What are the metrics that will be used to determine the success of the project?" Write down Jackson's answer and say, "Thank you."

SCRIPT 3: HIGH STAKES MEETINGS, YOUR OWN QUESTION

If you have done your research on the meeting, it's quite possible that you have come up with other questions you want to ask. Go for it! Just be sure to use the short script approach that I have taught you for the benchmarks and metrics questions: "*Name of speaker*, I have a question. *State your question.*" Listen to answer, write it down, and say, "Thank you."

STEP 3: WRITE DOWN WHAT HAPPENS NEXT.

Notice what happens to the other participants when you ask your question.

What are the likely outcomes?

First, I will tell you what isn't going to happen. Nobody is going to get up and walk out of the room like they did to me when I was in Saudi Arabia. So, you are already well ahead of the nightmare scenario I lived through!

What is more likely to happen is that one of the leaders in the room says, "Good question." But even if your question isn't acknowledged, you have met your goal of getting your voice heard. With more practice, you will soon feel confident enough to actively participate in any meeting.

STEP 4: EXECUTE.

Look at your calendar and select three upcoming meetings. Do the meeting prep to ask questions.

TRICKY SITUATION #3: HANDLING INTERRUPTERS AND IDEA STEALERS

Here is a place where gender differences are noteworthy.[32,33] Women on average are more frequently interrupted by men and by other women. Since this is such a common workplace occurrence, you need to have a strategy for managing it. Let me start by saying what not to do. I don't recommend you execute meeting jujitsu. You have probably read about it. A woman, usually a senior woman, will say the following: "When I get interrupted or my idea is stolen, I gently but firmly interrupt them and say, 'I am glad you agree with me' or 'That is what I just said.'"

This is bad advice.

First, it's difficult to execute. I don't know about you, but when I am in the middle of a meeting and my idea is stolen, I am usually too frustrated to say much of anything (my heart rate is going up, my vocal cords are constricting). So what actually comes out is the frustration. The gently-but-firmly part of the advice is thrown out the window. When you interrupt in a frustrated way, you just look hostile and petty. You reinforce the "emotional woman" stereotype and undermine yourself.

Second, it doesn't get the desired result. I have never been in a meeting where someone did that and the "perpetrator" said, "You are right, that was your idea, sorry about that." Usually, it's ignored.

You risk your ability to command respect for no result.

Instead, use your self-control and meeting techniques I have taught you. Take a deep breath, ask a question to get back into the conversation, then express your next good idea.

I know what you are thinking: *Giving up on my idea isn't commanding respect. That jerk who stole my idea needs to be called out.* Both of those points are valid. And they are the wrong things to be focusing on in this context. Here's why.

I call over thirty group meetings a week and participate in dozens more. When I call a meeting, it's because I have a problem, and I believe that taking people away from the focus of their main tasks to sit together with me is the only way to solve my problem. I want them to synergize, riff off each other, and help me come up with the answer together. The meeting isn't about getting a singular, good idea from an individual. If I had thought one person had the answer, I would have saved a lot of time and money by just asking them.

Since I am expecting a group conversation, I often don't notice a specific idea and who said it. What I do notice are the following behaviors:

Figure 14. Summary of Observable Meeting Behaviors

POSITIVE BEHAVIORS I NOTICE IN MEETINGS	NEGATIVE BEHAVIORS I NOTICE IN MEETINGS
When someone enhances the flow of the meeting by riffing and expanding on the ideas being considered.	When someone disrupts the flow of the meeting. For example, when they stop the discussion and bring the focus to themselves and pick a fight about idea attribution.
When someone contributes a lot. When they keep adding to the conversation.	When someone doesn't contribute. For example, because they are seething about their idea being stolen or having been interrupted and don't recover fast enough.
When someone takes accountability to follow up on an action item.	When someone misses an opportunity to step up and complete an action item.

As much as it might feel good in the moment to emphasize your contribution and call someone out, it puts you in the wrong mindset. It increases the likelihood that you are going to display negative meeting behaviors.

The meetings I call are about me and my problem, not you. Your mindset needs to be focused on helping me. You are much better off if you can recover and contribute more ideas. I know you have many of them. By doing so, you will be displaying the positive behaviors that get you noticed. The positive behaviors that get you invited back to more meetings.

If you want to be individually recognized for something, raise your hand for a follow-up action item. That shows me that you can take initiative and accountability. And, at least for my meetings, that is the only time I give people "credit" and write their name down. And in the follow-up meeting, you will have my undivided attention when you update me with the status of your action item using the communication techniques I will teach you in Chapter 4.

As far as calling out the jerk, after my meeting, you can do whatever you want.

And when you are the one calling the meeting, I suggest you use the technique I outline in Script 7: Stopping Meeting Interrupters, The Good Point, Gloria, Technique.

RECAP

In order to command respect, you must be heard. You must claim your voice and be ready and willing to use it in a variety of situations. You can do it by being prepared. Be prepared to promote your accomplishments so your peers and leaders know what you have done and what you can do. Be prepared to confidently show up at those important meetings by switching from a performing mindset to a learning mindset and have your questions ready. And be prepared to swiftly recover from interruptions to make sure you are constantly contributing.

FROM RESPECT TO ADMIRATION, BECOMING THE GO-TO SOURCE FOR STEM INSIGHTS

"I know you aren't the expert on this topic, but I need you to take the lead because you are the only one I can put in front of the CEO to explain everything. Jack* will go into way too much detail, and Mike* talks in circles."

—My last two bosses
(*Names have been changed to protect the innocent)

In this chapter, you will learn:
1. The most underrated skill in STEM: getting non-STEM people to understand you.
2. The STEM Insights Communication Framework.
3. How to generate the content for the framework.

THE MOST UNDERRATED SKILL IN STEM: GETTING NON-STEM PEOPLE TO UNDERSTAND YOU

Being the go-to person to share important insights with others has been the biggest differentiator in my career. Being the go-to person for these insights is a surefire way for you to command respect, too.

In my experience, experts, both men and women, are often perceived as poor communicators. I see this firsthand in my role as head of innovation, where I lead all the scientists and engineers. And when they try to have a conversation with sales, finance, or managers from other areas, problems ensue. At some point, very quickly in the conversation, the non-scientist will say, "This is too technical, get to the point." Or, "You are rambling, you lost me." In some cases, they will avoid the experts altogether, not wanting to be dragged down the rabbit hole of jargon. You can't command respect when people avoid you.

From my vantage point, this isn't a gendered issue at all. It's a communication issue. People only think you are rambling if you aren't saying anything interesting to them. How to communicate so that your audience will be interested in what you say is a teachable skill. I have taught this to my teams and at universities.

Now, I am going to teach you.

Here is what one student said about my approach:

> ### Dear Angelique,
>
> I have assumed the management of the process control team. I trained them on how to present to executives (based on your presentation), and the result was amazing! The manager liked it a lot and the team loved the way of sharing the project info. Thanks for sharing this with us!
>
> —ADOLFO

By the way, when I got this message, I logged it in my Small Wins Inventory. It was really nice to get positive feedback and to know that my coaching and mentoring was helping people.

An Example of how *NOT* to become the Go-to for STEM insights

Imagine you are a project leader named Sasha. You are giving a status update presentation to the head of sales on an important product development. You begin the presentation by saying, "I am here to talk to you about our exciting new product. We are currently on schedule with the development." So far, the head of sales is thinking, "That is good." Then you start to talk in detail about the characteristics of the product using technical equations.

$$Q = \frac{\pi \Delta p r^4}{8 \mu L}$$

Poiseuille's Law

You continue, "As you can see, with this product, the flow rate is much faster due to the viscosity . . ."

At this point, the executive is thinking, "Ugh! I have no idea what she is talking about. How can I get out of this conversation as quickly as possible?" After about two minutes, the head of sales finally says, "We are almost out of time, Sasha. Can you give me the thirty-second highlight of what you need us to know?" Feeling flustered, Sasha says, "Oh, sorry, as I said, we are on schedule, but we would like to increase the budget by twenty thousand dollars. I will send you a detailed proposal via email."

What just happened?

There are three problems. First, since Sasha didn't hook the audience with information that was relevant to them at the very beginning, the audience felt impatient as a result. Second, since Sasha used jargon that wasn't understood by her audience, they felt confused. Finally, Sasha didn't use her time wisely and didn't get to finish her presentation to ask for a larger budget.

Sasha didn't have the right approach to sharing the important points about her project.

Depending on your audience, in some cases, they will be sitting at the edge of their seats when you show them the scientific equations that underpin your results. Other times, they won't care less about the methodology you use to support your conclusions. And for all cases, you need to be aware of the amount of time you have and use it for maximum impact. In the next sections, I will go over a framework you can use to analyze your situation in advance and develop the most effective communication strategy.

THE STEM INSIGHTS COMMUNICATION FRAMEWORK

There are two components to analyzing your situation in order to determine your most effective approach: the context and the audience. Based on those two pieces of information, you can develop a strategy for creating and sharing the appropriate insights. I am going to tell you how to quickly analyze your situation and then develop the right content.

Here is the framework. As you can see, the framework is a 2x2 matrix. The two criteria to consider are the audience and the context. With that information, you have four different communication strategies to choose from.

Figure 15. The STEM Insights Communication Framework

High	Strategy #2	Strategy #3
Context Type		
Low	Strategy #1	Strategy #4
	Low	**High**

Audience Type

Context

The context is the environment in which you are speaking. Typical contexts include:

- One-on-one meeting
- Part of a bigger meeting
- Scientific conference
- In a conference room
- Passing a colleague in the hallway

The context is important because it can help you to determine how long you have to get your point across and what kind of medium you should use (verbal only, use of visual aids, etc.).

For our quick context analysis, what we want to know is if we will have a lot of time or a little bit of time.

EXERCISE 9: ANALYZE YOUR CONTEXT

How much time do I expect to have?

- More than ten minutes = High
- Less than ten minutes = Low
- If you aren't sure = Low

Audience

The audience is whom you are speaking with. Key questions you can ask yourself to better understand your audience include:[34]

1. Who is in this audience?

2. What opinions does your audience already have about the topic you are presenting?

3. Where are you addressing the audience? What things about the context or occasion might influence your audience members' interests and dispositions?

4. When are you addressing the audience? This is not just a matter of the time of day, but also why your topic is timely for the audience.

5. Why would your audience be interested in your topic? Why should these people make a particular judgment, change their minds, or take a specific action? In other words, how does your goal intersect with their interests, concerns, and aspirations?

For our quick audience analysis, you need to know if the audience has a high or low level of expertise on the topic on which you are speaking.

EXERCISE 10: ANALYZE YOUR AUDIENCE

Use these two guiding questions to analyze the level of subject matter expertise of your audience.

- Are the key members of your audience normally in the room with you during your team meetings?
- Do you normally consult with the key members of your audience for guidance on the details of your work?

Yes to both = High

No to either = Low

For our example of an executive briefing, we are going to assume that we have ten minutes and our audience has a low level of expertise in our topic. I place this situation in the framework in Figure 16.

Figure 16. STEM Insights Communication Framework,
Executive Briefing Example

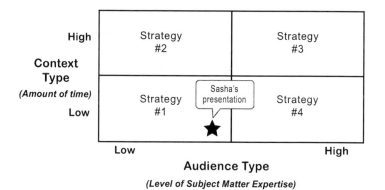

To make sure that you really understand this analysis, here is a summary of common situations we might find ourselves in and where they fit in the framework.

Figure 17. STEM Insights Communication Framework, Common Situations

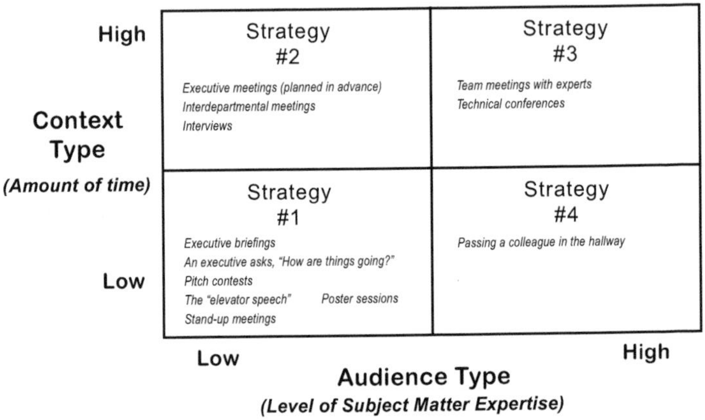

What you will notice is that in your day-to-day job, you are probably in situation #3. You are talking to other experts and you have more than ten minutes to do so. You will also notice that when you talk to anyone other than your direct peers, you need a different strategy to communicate your insights.

HOW TO GENERATE CONTENT FOR THE STEM INSIGHTS COMMUNICATION FRAMEWORK

Now we are ready to get into the details of how to create the content you will use for each of the strategies. The good news is that while we have four unique communication strategies to consider, they are all based on the same core information you already have. For a given project, there are five key elements. These are the basic components of any engineering project, scientific study, IT project, operational excelling project, etc. Below is a summary of the key elements and a description. For clarity, I've included some synonyms for each project element.

Figure 18. The Five Key Elements of a Project

PROJECT ELEMENT	DESCRIPTION
Current Condition (CC)	The situation as it is today, with respect to your focus area. Other words to describe this element are: *context* and *situation*.
Target Condition (TC)	Where you are trying to get to. Other words to describe this element are: *goals* and *objectives*.
Analysis (A)	Your analysis. Other words to describe this element are: *methodology* and *approach*.

PROJECT ELEMENT	DESCRIPTION
Results (R)	Your results to date. Other words to describe this element are: *status* and *findings*.
Next Steps (NS)	What you plan to do next, including finishing the work if it isn't finished and expanding your work to other areas of applicability. Other words to describe this element are: *future work* and *action plan*.

Just to convince yourself that you already have the core of what you need to become the go-to person to share insights, do the following exercise with an example project.

EXERCISE 11: SUMMARIZE YOUR KEY PROJECT ELEMENTS

You will need your workbook or one sheet of paper. On the paper, make two columns. Label the first column "Project Element" and the second column "Description." It should look like this:

Figure 19. The Five Key Elements of a Project Template

PROJECT ELEMENT	DESCRIPTION
Current Condition (CC)	
Target Condition (TC)	
Analysis (A)	
Results (R)	
Next Steps (NS)	

Using the guiding comments from Figure 18, fill in the elements for your own project.

Given that the basic facts about our work don't change, the insights strategies merely package the facts in the most effective way for the given situation. With that understanding, go back and look again at Figure 17. Can you see that for situations #3 and #4, we can package our facts using language for experts? For situations #1 and #2, we package our facts using language for nonexperts. For situations #2 and #3, we have time to elaborate on the facts; for situations #1 and #4, we don't have much time, so we must be succinct.

To further solidify the point, let's go back and think about Sasha's situation. We already mentioned that her audience had a low level of expertise on her topic and she had ten minutes to speak. Yet, she started to talk about Poiseuille's Law in detail (expert's language), and she ran out of time before she got to her most important point: asking for more money for the project (elaboration). If we look at the framework, we can have a better understanding of how her approach didn't fit her situation. She was inside her comfort zone and used strategy #3 when she should have been using strategy #2. I bet many of you can think of times when you did exactly the same thing.

Figure 20. Actual vs. Optimal Approach for Executive Briefing Example

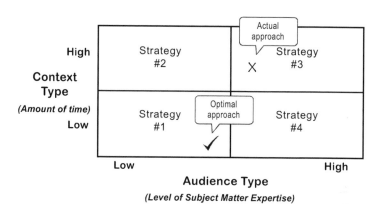

In the next sections, I will teach you how to transition from our default communication strategy (#3) to strategies for more common workplace situations (#1 and #2). In other words, I will teach you how to select the correct language and how to be succinct.

Selecting the right language for our audience

The most challenging task for those of us in STEM is to give up our expert language. It isn't challenging because we don't know the words to use. In fact, the words themselves are part of everyday language. We don't have to learn anything new. It's challenging because (1) expert language is our comfort zone, and (2) we're skeptical that it's actually the correct way to communicate.

Let me guess, you had at least one of these reactions to my recommendation to use non-expert language in workplace situations:

1. "If I don't demonstrate my mastery of the science, my audience won't think I am smart."

2. "I am a scientist/engineering/mathematician! I have been hired to talk about the technical details. If I don't, I am not doing my job."

3. "I shouldn't have to dumb it down for management; they should have a baseline level of knowledge on this important topic."

4. "Our executive is an engineer; they don't need me to simplify it for them."

Am I close?

I understand why you would be reluctant to give up the comfortable communication style you are used to. I promise you: these fears and assumptions are unfounded. As someone who is often a member of the audience in these situations (as an executive, poster session judge, and pitch contest judge) let me offer you some perspectives:

1. If we didn't think you were smart, we wouldn't have hired/selected you in the first place. You don't have to keep demonstrating it to us. Furthermore, not being able to tell that we don't understand you doesn't demonstrate that you are smart.

2. Your job is to give us insights, not to regurgitate your favorite technical stuff. Tune your insights to what we want. If we want more or specific details, we'll ask for

them.

3. Management has the skills required for managers. There are many people just like you who wish we better understood your domain expertise. Sorry, if we aren't going to use it regularly, we aren't going to learn it. We are relying on you to give us the insights we need to act upon.

4. Yes, some of us are engineers/scientists/mathematicians, etc. But we are using different skills now as managers. Don't assume we have retained mastery of subject matter expertise or that we continue to follow the latest advancements.

I hope I have convinced you. But if I haven't, you can rest assured that I am not asking you to completely stop using expert language. I am only asking you to use it strategically depending on your situation. In the table below, I show you a description of the two different types of language we can use for different situations.

Figure 21. Communication Project Information Based on Audience Level of Expertise

PROJECT ELEMENT	DESCRIPTION	INFORMATION TYPE	
		HIGH LEVEL OF EXPERTISE (Strategies #3 and #4)	LOW LEVEL OF EXPERTISE (Strategies #1 and #2)
Current Condition (CC)	The situation as it is today with respect to your focus area.	CONCEPTS AND TERMS: Threats and/or opportunities in terms of general concepts: People Money Environment Specific metrics related to expertise UNITS OF MEASURE: Varied and sometimes obscure.	CONCEPTS AND TERMS: Threats and/or opportunities in terms of general concepts: People Money Environment UNITS OF MEASURE: Money, time, volume, weights, temperature, etc.
Target Condition (TC)	Where you are trying to get to	Targets for the specific metrics, for example, increase, decrease, % change	Increase, decrease, % change of commonly used units: Money, time, volume, weights, temperature, etc.

PROJECT ELEMENT	DESCRIPTION	INFORMATION TYPE	
		HIGH LEVEL OF EXPERTISE (Strategies #3 and #4)	LOW LEVEL OF EXPERTISE (Strategies #1 and #2)
Analysis Methodology (A)	Your analysis	Detailed experimental and analytical methods with references	Overview of methods by type: laboratory experiments, simulation, data analytics.
Results (R)	Your results to date	Raw data in obscure units. Schedule Budget (if applicable)	Increase, decrease, % change of commonly used units: Money, time, volume, weights, temperature, etc. Schedule (on time or not) Budget (on budget or not)
Next Steps (NS)	What you plan to do next	Summary of your next actions, with a timeline.	

Now, practice spotting the difference between expert and non-expert language.

EXERCISE 12: IDENTIFYING EXPERT VS. NON-EXPERT LANGUAGE

STEP 1. READ YOUR SUMMARY FROM EXERCISE 10.

STEP 2. IDENTIFY NON-EXPERT LANGUAGE.

Circle all non-expert phrases and metrics in your summary using the descriptions from Figure 21.

Do you have at least one metric circled in each category?

STEP 3. COMPLETE YOUR SUMMARY WITH NONEXPERT LANGUAGE.

Brainstorm possible descriptions and metrics you can use to make sure each element of your project summary has been covered.

Now you know how to use the appropriate language for strategies.

Selecting the right project elements to fit the allotted time

The second challenge we have is to make sure that we have enough time to communicate our main points about the project. For that, I will introduce two new concepts: a call to action (CTA) and the bottom line up front statement (BLUF).[35], [36]

A CTA is a sentence or two indicating what you want your audience to do with the information you are giving them during your discussion. Do you want them to be informed, decide on something, provide you with more resources, etc.? For the purposes of building our communication strategy, I will add the CTA to our Key Project Elements.

Figure 22. Key Project Elements with Call to Action

PROJECT ELEMENT	DESCRIPTION
Current Condition (CC)	The situation as it is today, with respect to your focus area. Other words to describe this element are: *context* and *situation*.
Target Condition (TC)	Where you are trying to get to. Other words to describe this element are: *goals* and *objectives*.
Analysis (A)	Your analysis. Other words to describe this element are: *methodology* and *approach*.

PROJECT ELEMENT	DESCRIPTION
Results (R)	Your results to date. Other words to describe this element are: *status* and *findings*.
Next Steps (NS)	What you plan to do next, including finishing the work if it isn't finished and expanding your work to other areas of applicability. Other words to describe this element are: *future work* and *action plan*.
Call to Action (CTA)	What do you want your audience to do with the information you are giving them? Examples include: decide something, approve something, provide additional resources.

With the CTA, you now have a complete summary of all the core pieces of information you want to communicate to your audience. It's a lot of information, so how could you possibly communicate everything in less than ten minutes? You can't. But you can be very deliberate about what you do communicate and optimize your time for maximum impact. That is where the BLUF statement comes in. The BLUF statement is a short paragraph in nonexpert language that captures the main point from each of your project elements.

If you refer back to, Figure 22, you can see that the BLUF statement can be constructed as follows:

Equation 1: STEM Insights BLUF Statement

STEM Insights BLUF Statement = CC+TC+A+R+NS+CTA

[all in nonexpert language]

I will illustrate how to do it with our example. Below is a summary of the key project elements for Sasha's project.

Figure 23. Key Project Elements in Non-expert Language
for Executive Briefing Example

PROJECT ELEMENT	DESCRIPTION	SASHA'S PROJECT
Current Condition (CC)	There is this problem/ gap or opportunity in my focus area	Revenue increase by 10% by developing product X.
Target Condition (TC)	Where you are trying to get to	Product X completed by January 2021.
Analysis Methodology (A)	Your analysis methodology	Laboratory testing and simulation.
Results (R)	Your results to date	Late due to simulation. On budget. Product properties are better than the competition with respect to flow rate.
Next Steps (NS)	What you plan to do next	In the next 3 months, we will complete the lab testing and simulation.
Audience call to action(CTA)	What do you want your audience to do with the information you are giving them?	Increase budget by $20k to outsource the analysis of the simulation data so that we can get back on schedule.

With each element, we can make the BLUF statement for her project:

> "We have an opportunity to increase our revenue by 10 percent by developing product X. We would like to have product X completed by January 2021. We are analyzing the features of product X using a combination of laboratory testing and simulation. We are currently behind schedule due to a delay in the development of the simulation. We are on budget. We see that the product properties are better than the competition with respect to flow rate. In the next three months, we will complete the lab testing and simulation. I am requesting twenty thousand dollars to outsource the analysis of the simulation data so that we can get back on schedule."

We can see in this statement that all of the project elements have been mentioned. We have raised the issue of needing more resources. It took me approximately sixty seconds to read it, thus leaving time for Q&A.

Any number of questions could arise from this summary. Depending on what the questions are, Sasha should be prepared to use expert or non-expert language to reply. For example:

Figure 24. Examples of How to Handle Q&A

POSSIBLE QUESTION	TYPE OF ANSWER
Tell me more about the features of the product	Expert language
Tell me more about your analysis methods	Expert language
Tell me more about the competition	Non-expert language
Tell me what you will use the $20k for	Non-expert language

EXERCISE 13: CREATING YOUR OWN STEM INSIGHTS BLUF STATEMENT

You will need your workbook or one sheet of paper. Label the page "BLUF Statement" and make two columns. The first column is labeled "Project Element" and the second column is labeled "Description." It should look like this:

Figure 25. STEM Insights BLUF Creator Template

PROJECT ELEMENT	DESCRIPTION	MY KEY ELEMENTS IN NON-EXPERT LANGUAGE
Current Condition (CC)	There is this problem/ gap or opportunity in my focus area	
Target Condition (TC)	Where you are trying to get to	
Analysis Methodology (A)	Your analysis methodology	
Results (R)	Your results to date	
Next Steps (NS)	What you plan to do next	
Audience call to action(CTA)	What do you want your audience to do with the information you are giving them?	

STEP 1: FILL IN THE TABLE WITH WHAT YOU KNOW ABOUT THE PROJECT.

I recommend you continue to develop the same project from Exercise 11.

STEP 2: ANALYZE YOUR AUDIENCE.

STEP 3: CHECK TO SEE IF YOU HAVE THE RIGHT LANGUAGE FOR YOUR AUDIENCE.

Here are some guiding questions:

- Have I described the problem, current conditions, and target conditions in general or highly specific terms?
- Have I described the methodology in terms of broad process steps or detailed methodologies?
- Have I described the results in general or highly specific terms? Have I mentioned the schedule and budget?
- Have I defined the next steps in general or highly specific terms?

STEP 4: GENERATE THE STEM INSIGHTS BLUF STATEMENT.

Create a short summary of six to ten sentences that describe each item in the BLUF statement.

$$CC+TC+A+R+NS+CTA$$

Putting it all together

Now that you have all the components of your STEM insights, we can build the strategy based on the situation we are in.

1. Strategy #1. Communicate your BLUF statement. Pause for questions. Answer questions in the type of language they are asked (expert vs non-expert).

2. Strategy# 2. Communicate your BLUF statement. Pause for questions. Answer questions in the type of language they are asked (expert vs non-expert). If time remains, elaborate on the most relevant key project elements.

3. Strategy #3. Communicate a summary of your key project elements in expert language. Pause for questions. Answer questions.

4. Strategy #4. Communicate the most relevant key project element in expert language.

If we return to our STEM insights strategy chart, it will look like this.

Figure 26. STEM Insights Communication Strategies with Explanations

High **Context Type** *(Amount of time)* **Low**	**Insights Strategy #2** *BLUF statements* *Followed by Q&A* *Followed by elaboration of key project elements*	**Insights Strategy #3** *Summary of key project elements in expert language* *Followed by Q&A* *Followed by elaboration of key project elements*
	Insights Strategy #1 *BLUF statement* *Followed by Q&A*	**Insights Strategy #4** *Most relevant key project element in expert language*

    Low   **High**

Audience Type

(Level of Subject Matter Expertise)

Frequently Asked Questions

1. How do I find the best metrics for my BLUF?

    a. Ask your boss or peers.

    b. Do detective work. Read publications from your target audience to find out what they care about. Annual reports, status reports, newsletters, etc. All of these have clues.

2. What if I have given a status update recently? Can I skip the BLUF statement?

    c. Unless recently means the last 48 hours, no. You need to analyze your audience. If your audience is low expertise, then stick to your communication strategy. First, your past presentation, as brilliant as I am sure it was, did not turn your audience into an expert. Second, your audience has probably seen tens if not hundreds of other projects since the last update. It's likely that they didn't retain the key points in your BLUF statement or summary and that a quick review will be beneficial for them. Otherwise, they will be confused.

3. Do I have to keep the BLUF statement elements in the same order?

   d. No. In fact an advanced technique would be to reorder your BLUF based on the priorities of your audience. For example, if you know that the audience is highly concerned about the schedule, you can say the line about the schedule first.

RECAP

The most underrated skill in STEM is getting non-STEM people to understand you. Mastering this skill has been a huge contributor to my own success. It's the number-one skill that I get asked to teach. I have provided a framework for analyzing your context and audience and developing a communication strategy that will work in any situation. The most important part is to remember that in most situations, you have to use the language of the nonexpert. Practice it, and you will quickly become the go-to person to explain all this STEM information.

THE THIRD KEY:

HOW TO CONTROL YOUR CAREER PATH

CHAPTER 5

FIGURING OUT YOUR NEXT CAREER MOVE

*"Management champions certain people,
and if you aren't chosen, you are left in the dust."*

—BRENDA

In this chapter, you will learn:
1. Why you shouldn't rely on your organization to help you with your career.
2. How to identify your next opportunity.
3. How to determine when you will be ready for your dream job.

WHY YOU SHOULDN'T RELY ON YOUR ORGANIZATION TO HELP YOU WITH YOUR CAREER

> "My organization doesn't help me. There was no one to follow, no one to tell me what it would be like and provide advice."
>
> —LYDIA

Are you frustrated that your organization doesn't do enough to help you chart a career path? You are not alone. According to the Mercer 2020 Global Talent Trends report which surveyed over 7,300 employees, 55 percent of people believe they don't have sufficient opportunity to advance in their current firm. Fifty-three percent feel like their firm does not have adequate structures to help them navigate a career change.[37] When I polled the eighty members of my Lady Visitor Project LinkedIn group, the statistics were even worse. None, as in 0 percent of the women I polled, had help from their organization to chart their career path.

Figure 27. Survey: Do You Know How to Make Your Next Career Move?

Do you know how to make your next career move?
You can see how people vote. Learn more

Yes, with help from my org.	0%
Yes, on my own. ⊘	50%
No.	50%

On top of that, firms that do have structured career path programs often focus on the development of so-called high-potential employees (HiPos). According to Harvard, "High potentials consistently and significantly outperform their peer groups in a variety of settings and circumstances. While achieving these superior levels of performance, they exhibit behaviors that reflect their companies' culture and values in an exemplary manner. Moreover, they show a strong capacity to grow and succeed throughout their careers within an organization—more quickly and effectively than their peer groups do."[38]

It makes sense for firms to focus limited development dollars on employees who they believe can generate the highest return on investment. The problem is whether it be the path or the pace, the model of the traditional career progression doesn't work for most women or men.[39] The idea of the individual contributor who works long hours and becomes a manager, takes an international assignment, then becomes a director, and then an executive leader in ten years is outdated. There are many people who don't want to be managers. Also, in the first ten years of a career, many people choose to start a family. It's widely known that women take on more of such childcare duties.

I experienced this firsthand as a manager. I will never forget my first performance discussion. When it was time to discuss a young woman in our team who had received glowing reviews from internal and external customers and the team, her manager said, "I think she should get a high rating and bonus for this year, but we should not consider her as a HiPo. I don't want to invest in her development because she is probably going to get married, have kids, and leave in a few years." I was shocked by this. It was so outdated. And ironic, since I had just taken over the role of his boss when I returned only weeks earlier from maternity leave. Fortunately, I was able to use my power to promote her anyway. I think my exact words were: "Get her promotion package on my desk in two weeks." She did a great job.

Nearly ten years later, the problem persists. I am still sitting in talent review meetings where there are questions about what we do with the HiPos who don't want to move or work ninety hours a week.

What about those employee resource groups (ERGs)? Do your peers or more senior women show you the ropes and help you get ahead? The evidence is mixed. When I interviewed the eighty women in my Lady Visitor Project LinkedIn group, only 50 percent said they found their organization's women's network helpful. Many of them left the group after a while.

Figure 28. Survey: How Helpful Is Your Workplace Women's Network?

Workplace Women's Networks
You can see how people vote. Learn more

| Very helpful. | 50% |
| Not useful for me. ⊘ | 50% |

"Workplace women's networks don't work. The women who have made it don't want to share their insights; they are 'stingy.' There is not a feeling of safety in the group due to 'lack of trust' and 'competition.'"

—MELANIE

In hindsight, I can see how junior women might not get much out of it. I always participated in my workplace women's network, seeing it mostly as a place for me to use my leadership skills that weren't being used in my actual job. I also wanted to get access to leaders in different departments. I was focused on what was in it for me and didn't spend a lot of time mentoring other women.

I didn't realize this until I was at an offsite with a mentee. I think because I already knew that I was leaving the company, I was feeling a bit more open about discussing my past experiences. When the subject of gender discrimination came up, I told her about a couple of examples that had happened to me and how I handled them. The next day, she came up to me and said that was the best discussion she had ever had in her career. Knowing that things had also happened to me and how I handled them was helpful. She wasn't alone, and now she had some idea of what she could try.

I was thrilled that I had helped her, but I also thought to myself, *Why hadn't I ever said those things to anyone before?* The first reason: fear. I was afraid that I would get tagged as a troublemaker if it got out that I was talking about these experiences. Let's face it, there are not many examples of women making it to the top of their organizations by throwing shade at their male peers.

The second reason: shame. I was ashamed to say that things had happened to me and that I hadn't raised hell. I was a fraud to be considered a champion for women when sometimes I didn't even stick up for myself.

The bottom line: Your workplace has little to offer you to support your career advancement. Most firms don't adequately invest in career development resources. Those that do often apply an overly narrow view of who is worthy of receiving those resources. If you have chosen to take a slower path or to temporarily get off the fast track, you will be left behind. And peer groups often don't provide the environments needed for women to share what it's really like and what it really takes to get back on track.

What all this means is that if you want to define a career path, you are on your own. The good news is that with some effort and an action plan, you can design a career roadmap that you control. Here is how to do it.

HOW TO IDENTIFY YOUR NEXT CAREER OPPORTUNITY

> "I think that in my last company, you were only defined as being a 'success' if you decided to be in a role that managed people. I always felt like a failure because this is not where my interest lies. So, I left."
>
> —CRYSTAL

If you happen to be one of those people who already knows exactly what they want to do, you can skip to the next section "How to determine if you are ready for your dream job." But if you are like me and are not really sure, you need to embark on an exploration process. The single best way I have found to get a good idea of what a job might be like is to ask people who are already doing it via informational interviews.

Informational interviews are a simple tool to collect firsthand information about a work environment or specific role you might be interested in. Even if you have no idea about what you are interested in, you can start talking to people to collect data.

There are a few things that make people reluctant to conduct informational interviews. I am going to tell you how to overcome those challenges and give you scripts you can use.

Challenge #1: Making the ask

Asking for help is intimidating. Put yourself in the learning mindset and remember that this conversation is going to help you define the path for your career. The key to asking someone to grant you an informational interview is to be polite, prepared, and succinct. Below is a basic script for requesting the interview.

SCRIPT 4: INFORMATIONAL INTERVIEWS, MAKING THE ASK

Hello *their Name*,

I am thinking about the next step in my career, and I am interested in learning more about what you do. Can we schedule a one-hour meeting at your convenience to talk?

Here are a few of my questions:

Question 1

Question 2

Question 3

Thanks in advance for your consideration.

Best Regards,

Your name

I have made this ask dozens of times, and I have never had anyone turn me down. It's only an hour, and I have prepared my questions in advance so the other person knows what to expect. Similarly, when I've been asked to be interviewed, I have been nothing but flattered. My only hesitation has been when I didn't get any questions in advance, and I would spend some time wondering what they were going to ask me. So don't do that; include at least a few questions in the email.

SCRIPT 5: INFORMATIONAL INTERVIEWS, ASKING FOR A REFERRAL

If you don't already know the person to whom you will be speaking, you can request that someone you know make a referral on your behalf. I have found that the easiest way to get someone to refer you is to do all of the work for them. In that case, you might need to send two notes. Send the first message to the person you know, asking for a referral. Send the second message to your target interviewee.

> Hello *Name of person who will make the referral*,
>
> I am thinking about the next step in my career, and I am interested in learning more about what *target interviewee* does. I would like to schedule a meeting with them. Can you arrange an introduction for me? I have included a message you could forward along if you want.
>
> Thanks in advance for your help.

* * * *

Hello target interviewee's Name,

My colleague your name is your current role.

She is exploring career options and is interested in learning a bit more about what you do.

Do you mind if I make an email introduction between the two of you?

Thanks,

Challenge #2: What should I ask?

You need to focus on what will be important for you to know about the job in three critical areas:

1. Skills (specific competencies that are required to do the job)
2. Incentives (how the job is funded, metrics used to evaluate performance)
3. Environment (day-to-day life)

One mistake that people make is only asking questions that help them learn if they are capable of doing the job. You also need to ask questions about whether or not you would want to do the job.

When I knew that I was no longer going to pursue an executive role in my old firm, I started to look around. At first, I was convinced that I wanted to go into academia. I have always enjoyed teaching. I was spending my weekends at MIT, and the professors seemed to be having a really good time.

I conducted four informational interviews at several universities. What I learned quickly changed my mind. There is a class system in academia. The upper class is the researcher track (writes grants and scientific publications). The lower class is the senior lecturer track (teaches and writes books). If I wanted to be in the upper class, where the real money is (unless you happen to write a viral best seller), it would be extremely difficult and would require me to almost start over.

Then, there was an issue with the incentives. In academia, generating value is measured in the form of publications and research grants. Whereas in the corporate world, value is measured based on currency—how much money did you save the company or how much revenue did you generate? I am much more motivated by the incentives in the corporate environment. I decided to stay corporate. But I also decided to teach. I lecture on innovation both inside my firm and at universities.

Challenge #3: What do I say to my manager?

If you want to conduct informational interviews within your firm, I recommend you tell your manager about it. Keeping open and transparent communication with your manager is always the recommended action.

SCRIPT 6: INFORMATIONAL INTERVIEWS, WHAT TO SAY TO YOUR MANAGER

Hi *your manager's name,*

I am thinking about my career development. I have noticed that target *interviewee 1* and *interviewee 2* are doing some interesting things, and I plan to talk with them about their work.

Anyone else you can think of that could be good for me to talk to?

Your Name

Most of the time, your message will be positively viewed. You are taking a proactive approach to your own career development. The most likely outcome will be a comment like "Good idea, let me know if I can help." Unfortunately, this approach is not totally without risk. It's possible that you have a manager who has other ideas about what your career should look like and might bristle at the fact that you are being proactive. I recommend you do it anyway.

If your boss has trouble with you having a conversation with someone in the organization, they are probably causing you other issues that you will need to deal with in the future. I had a manager tell me that I was being too ambitious thinking that I deserved to be talking to the chief technology officer. I had multiple problems with this person and was eventually able to get out of his organization.

On the other hand, if you are planning to talk to people <u>outside</u> of your firm, I recommend that you don't disclose it. There is absolutely nothing wrong with doing it. Any professional in this day and age is expected to always be exploring opportunities. Even though this is just an information-gathering exercise, you don't need to call attention to yourself.

Remember: You are being interviewed, too

Any good manager is always scouting for talent. That means that when you arrange the informational interview, you need to recognize that you are also being interviewed a little bit, too.[40] Don't worry! It just means you need to have the right mindset and prepare a little bit in advance. You are already making a good impression by reaching out proactively. And you already have your questions ready. Now you need to be prepared for their questions.

There are a few basic things that you could be asked. Just make a few notes on these topics, and you will have a very productive discussion.

1. What do you do? (a one-minute self-introduction)
2. What interested you in coming to talk to me?
3. When do you think you are going to be ready to make the next move?

For question #3, I suggest that you be vague. Unless you have already discussed a timeline with your boss, it's best to say something like, "I am just exploring." You don't want to have your boss be surprised in an HR discussion that you told another manager you were ready to move right away. Causing an embarrassing moment for your manager is a quick way to lose their support.

Finally, remember to send a thank-you note via email.

HOW TO DETERMINE IF YOU ARE READY FOR YOUR DREAM JOB

> "I would see those positions but never apply, feeling I was not good enough yet, despite having sixteen-plus years of experience in management."
>
> —SATYA

Once you have conducted some informational interviews, you will start to understand the kinds of roles that you might be interested in. The next step is to get some clarity on when they will be a good fit for you. Notice I say when, not if. I truly believe in the mantra of the Khan Academy: You can learn anything.[41] I also believe that you are good enough to do what you want. Remember, we covered that in Chapter 1. You may not have the skills and network now, but you can get it. With those two fundamental truths as the basis, you do need to be clear on what it will take, and then you can decide if you want to go after it or not.

It can be helpful to consider if the role is a fit for you now or later. To make that determination, I am going to show you how to analyze job descriptions.

EXERCISE 14: JOB QUALIFICATIONS ANALYSIS

For this activity, you need the accomplishments list you completed in Exercise 1. If you are interested in a job that is already posted, you can use that description. If you are just starting to explore, you can find detailed job descriptions on the internet.

STEP 1: GET JOB DESCRIPTIONS FOR ROLES OF INTEREST.

I like to use Indeed.com (USA only) or LinkedIn.com (global) to find job descriptions.

Below is an example of a typical job description. They generally follow the same structure: a description of the firm, a set of responsibilities, the qualifications, and the benefits. Each of the elements might be in a different sequence, but they are all present in a well-written job description.

Here is an example for a chief diversity, equity, and inclusion officer role:

Figure 29. Example Job Description

FULL JOB DESCRIPTION

A quick summary about the Chief Diversity, Equity, and Inclusion role:
The Chief Diversity, Equity, and Inclusion Officer leads the development and implementation of proactive diversity, equity, inclusion initiatives in alignment with the company's strategic goals to create and nurture a climate that is welcoming, inclusive, respectful, and free from discrimination, intolerance, and harassment.

What the Chief Diversity, Equity, and Inclusion Officer will do:
Provide strong leadership in leading overall Diversity, Equity, and Inclusion strategies and execution for the company. Key focus areas include:

CULTURE AND VALUES:
- Create and expand our initial strategic roadmap for diversity, equity, and inclusion into a robust plan that aligns with our diversity and inclusion goals.
- Build and foster a culture of diversity, equity, and inclusion through innovative programs and initiatives that build awareness, partnerships, and capabilities across the organization while enhancing both the employee and candidate experience

ENGAGEMENT AND RETENTION
- Be a contributing member of the Social Justice Task Force and provide guidance and direction to the task for team members and workstreams.
- Develop opportunities to connect and engage recently recruited and hired diverse team members within the community.
- Identify KPIs and develop an approach to assess progress achievement and accountability within the organization and partner with the People Team (HR) to measure the impact and effectiveness of diversity, equity, and inclusion initiatives and the overall impact on culture and the employee experience.
- Implement and execute an ongoing DEI organization-wide assessment to identify gaps and areas of continued development.

HIRING AND PROMOTION EQUITY
- Partner with the Talent Acquisition to create a detailed plan to help to continue to identify and recruit top talent with nontraditional backgrounds to drive innovation and leverage their unique assets to advance the objectives of the organization.
- Develop a talent management framework for identifying and grooming high-potential, high-performing diverse team members that aligns with best practices for organizational retention and promotional practices.

LEARNING AND DEVELOPMENT
- Provide subject matter expertise, coaching, and education with our executive and senior leadership team to align the organizational strategy to advance functional and key business outcomes.

- Utilize and promote internal affinity groups to strengthen employee collaboration and support.

DIVERSIFIED PARTNERSHIPS
- Strategically align with outside organizations to help augment our strategy and push beyond "best practices" to innovate and create groundbreaking thought-leadership.
- Manage key nonpolitical community relationships with an emphasis on partnering with other appropriate internal leaders and teams to advance the organization's brand as it relates to social responsibility, community partners, key stakeholders, and diversity programs.

SUPPLIER AND VENDOR RELATIONS
- Build and establish relationships in business communities to create learning and development, employee engagement, and retention opportunities.
- Implement policies, processes, technology, communication, and training to assure identification, qualification, and inclusion of diverse suppliers.
- Develop and execute an outreach strategy to build extensive diverse supplier relationships and create internal and external networking opportunities to connect diverse suppliers with business stakeholders.

GENERAL RESPONSIBILITIES
- Provide support, as necessary, to all business units including game day, events, and business operations.
- In conjunction with executive leadership, formulate and carry out company policies, objectives, and programs.
- Deal with complex factors not easily evaluated and make decisions based on conclusions for which there may be little precedent.

REQUIRED QUALIFICATIONS
- 10+ years of experience planning, designing, and delivering programs and practices related to diversity and inclusion.
- A proven record of strategic leadership in planning, developing, evaluating, and implementing diversity strategies designed to strengthen and improve the work environment.
- Interpersonal skills to build lasting relationships and drive consensus.

- Proven track record of developing diversity and inclusion frameworks.
- Deep understanding of concepts related to diversity, equity, and inclusion.
- Outstanding creative thinking skills.
- Ability to meet tight deadlines and work well under pressure.
- Strong synergy skills.
- Strong organizational skills.
- Strong verbal and written communication skills.
- Ability to prioritize and manage multiple projects.
- Ability to work independently.
- Strong project management skills.
- Excellent ability to establish rapport with others.
- Willingness to work a flexible schedule.

WHAT WE OFFER
- Competitive compensation plan.
- 35 days of paid time off (personal days and holidays).
- Medical, dental, and vision benefits.
- 401k with company match.

STEP 2: IDENTIFY THE QUALIFICATIONS FOR THE ROLE OF INTEREST.

Find the qualifications section of the job description. The section we are interested in might have the following title:

- Qualifications
- What the role needs to have
- The role requires
- Knowledge skills and experience required

You can find the fifteen qualifications in our example job description under the heading: "Required Qualifications."

STEP 3: IDENTIFY THE ACCOMPLISHMENTS YOU HAVE THAT MATCH THE QUALIFICATIONS.

Review your accomplishments list and count how many of your accomplishments match the qualifications.

There are a couple of things to note:

- One of the qualifications usually pertains to the number of years of experience required. If you are within three years of that, consider it an accomplishment that matches the job description. In other words, if the job description says you must have ten years of experience and you have seven, you should count it toward your number of qualifications. If you only have five years in the role, don't count it.
- Your accomplishments can count for more than one qualification. In other words, if you have an accomplishment that demonstrates both creative thinking (qualification #6) and your ability to work independently (qualification #12), then you should count it twice.

STEP 4: ANALYZE HOW WELL YOUR CREDENTIALS MATCH THE ROLE.

Once you have counted the number of accomplishments you have for the role, you need to determine if you are a fit for the role.

Equation 2: Role Fit Index (RFI)

I HAVE CLASSIFIED THE FIT AS FOLLOWS:

- RFI > 0.7, you are *ready now* for the role.
- RFI < 0.5, you are *ready later* for the role.
- RFI .51–.69, you are *almost ready* for the role.

Notice that a ready-now role does not mean an RFI of 1. Having 100 percent of the qualifications for a role is an unreasonable expectation. Hiring managers often have only a vague notion of what they really want. And translating that into the rigid format of an HR job description is difficult.[42] Also, studies show that men are confident about their ability at 60 percent, but women don't feel confident until they've checked off each item on the list.[43] If you wait for 100 percent, you will miss out.

STEP 4: ANALYZE AT LEAST FIVE JOB DESCRIPTIONS.

Make sure that you have a large enough sample size of job descriptions by analyzing at least five.

Based on your analysis, I outline the appropriate next steps in Chapter 6.

RECAP

You are on your own when it comes to your career. HR has limited resources to help you. You can take charge by learning about opportunities inside and outside of your current organization with informational interviews. You can take an objective view of how close you are to landing your dream job by analyzing job descriptions and calculating the role fit index.

HOW TO GET READY FOR YOUR DREAM JOB AND GET IT

"I feel so disappointed currently with the direction my career has gone, especially recent events of a reorg that left me totally questioning my career and why I even bothered."

—ASHLEY

In this chapter, you will learn:
1. What to do if you aren't ready for your dream role.
2. What to do if you are ready for your dream role.
3. What to do if you aren't actively looking.

WHAT TO DO IF YOU AREN'T READY FOR YOUR DREAM JOB

If you find that your current qualifications don't match the profile of your dream job, you have two options.

1. Find something else.
2. Develop a plan to close the gaps.

Both are viable pathways.

Referring to my example of being interested in academia, I decided that the skills gap was too large, and the incentives didn't match my interests. I chose not to pursue it. If you chose to pursue a dream job that requires you to complete a development plan, below is a summary of how to approach it.

Figure 30: Summary of Approaches to Closing Development Gaps

DEVELOPMENT APPROACH	DESCRIPTION	ADVANTAGES (+) DISADVANTAGES (-)	HOW TO FIND AN OPPORTUNITY
Learn-by-doing inside your firm	Take on a project inside your current organization that will require you to learn the skills that you currently lack.	+ If you succeed, it will give you the most direct credibility. + You will have an accomplishment to add to your list and your firm will endorse it because it benefited them. - It can be difficult to find such a project.	Ask your boss for a development opportunity

DEVELOPMENT APPROACH	DESCRIPTION	ADVANTAGES (+) DISADVANTAGES (-)	HOW TO FIND AN OPPORTUNITY
Learn-by-doing outside your firm	Take on a project outside your organization that will require you to learn the skills you currently lack.	+ If you succeed, you will have an accomplishment to add to your list. - It may be difficult to translate the external experience to your target organization.	Volunteer in a nonprofit, advise a start-up, or join a board.
Take a course	Take a course in the target topic.	+ Generally easy to find. - Can be expensive. - Depending on the course, it may not offer an accomplishment you can put on your list. - Your target organization might not value training.	Check your local university or online resources for courses.

I recommend learn-by-doing approaches when they are available. Taking on a project that forces you to experience the skills that are needed to close your development gaps is the most direct way to show potential employers that you can do it. Learn-by-doing projects also give you the opportunity to test out the situation. You might find that you don't actually like doing that kind of work. Or you might find that you are naturally skilled at it. If you are shuddering at the idea of taking on a new project, I have an approach for you in Chapter 7.

Training approaches are also possible. You can identify the right classes to fill your skill gaps. Your firm may even pay for it. Invariably, someone on my staff will request external training. With tight budgets, it can be extremely difficult for a manager to fund such activities. Even if you are fortunate to have a training budget, as is the case in many places in Europe, it's still a good idea to put together a short proposal. To increase your chances of success, I will share with you the external training proposal checklist that I make all my people complete if they want to ask me for money. Remember that I work in a corporate environment, so if you are in a different setting, you might have to adapt it.

CHECKLIST 1: EXTERNAL TRAINING REQUEST

- Is this training required for your career progression?
- What evidence can you provide to support the need?
- Does this support an existing project or strategic lever?
- Have you checked our internal training programs to see if you can get this for free?
- Have you shopped around for at least three proposals to ensure we are getting the best value for our money?
- What do you plan to do differently once you have this training?

WHAT TO DO IF ARE READY OR ALMOST READY FOR YOUR DREAM JOB

Apply!

Whether your role fit index indicates you are ready now or almost ready, I suggest you follow the instructions below for the ready-now role. For almost-ready roles, you need to be realistic. Apply and see what kind of feedback you get. If you don't get any response, you can consider that you have gaps and then you can put that kind of role in your ready-later category.

Before you apply, you need to make sure that your LinkedIn profile and resume are ready.

Updating your LinkedIn profile

If you are not already on LinkedIn, you should be. Any professional who wants to build her network or potentially look for a job must be on LinkedIn. If you apply for a job, you can be certain that the HR recruiter and possibly the hiring manager will check your profile.

There is a lot of information available on how to make a good profile.[44, 45] Below is the minimum that you should do for your profile:

CHECKLIST 2: LINKEDIN PROFILE MINIMUM REQUIREMENTS

1. Up-to-date profile picture
2. Title
3. Brief description of what you have done and would like to do in the About Section.
4. List of previous roles and activities using your Accomplishments Inventory in the Experience Section
5. Your education in the Education Section
6. Your profile should be free of spelling and grammatical errors

In addition to the absolute minimum I recommend above, I think a more advanced, but well worth it, enhancement to your profile is a very thoughtful summary.[46] This is a place to bring your personality into your profile.

"I must have revised my profile summary at least 5 times. Once I got it how I really wanted it, I started to get approached for the right jobs."

—SHARON

At the time of this writing, I have the profile summary below. I have had many people reach out to me because, in it, I mention that my passion is helping innovators turn their ideas into value.

> I am an experienced innovation executive with expertise in all aspects of development from ideation to commercialization. I have a proven track record of leading functionally and geographically diverse organizations to overachieve goals. Having spent most of my career in the global manufacturing environment, I am adept at influencing stakeholders from the C-suite to the shop floor. My passion is helping innovators turn their ideas into value.

LinkedIn profile advice that I think is okay to skip is everything related to images, videos, and other items that focus on aesthetics. Unless aesthetics are directly related to a job you are seeking, you don't have to worry about it.

Creating or updating your LinkedIn profile can be scary, especially for those of us who are not used to living our lives online for everyone to see. I remember eagerly putting my first LinkedIn profile up and trying to get connections. It was fun and exciting. But when I realized that I wanted to change my profile to be more assertive in my accomplishments, the self-doubt started to creep back in. What if my colleagues saw it and disagreed with what I wrote or thought I was being boastful?

Fortunately, LinkedIn has some built-in features that allow people like us to take it slowly if we need to. At the time of this writing, here is how to do it.

In your profile:
> Privacy settings → Visibility → Visibility of your LinkedIn Activity → Share job changes, education changes, and work anniversaries from your profile.

You can get there directly from this URL: https://www.
linkedin.com/psettings/activity-broadcast

If this process has changed, you can Google "LinkedIn
privacy settings," and LinkedIn will provide you with
updates.

Figure 31: LinkedIn Privacy Settings for Profile Changes.

Resume Writing and Interviewing

Resume writing and interviewing are very important
topics, and detailed treatments are beyond the scope of this
book. When you are ready for that, I strongly recommend
the guidance provided by the team at Manager-tools.com.
I have listened to their podcasts and held a license for their
premium content for over ten years. I find their advice to
be spot on and highly actionable. The best part is it's free.
Just do what they recommend. That is what I did, with great
success.

I tried my best to follow the Manager-tools.com
resume-writing advice.[47] I show you a version of my resume
below. A few general notes:

1. Notice that I use the exact structure we discussed in Exercise 2: The Accomplishments Inventory. After the title of each role and a brief description of my duties, I list my accomplishments as bullets. "Achieved _____ by doing _____." Or "Accomplished _____ through _____."

2. Plan to make more than one resume. It's much better to customize your resume for the job description than to try to cram everything on your resume. I have had resumes targeting research, strategy, and operational excellence roles.

Figure 32: Example Resume

ANGELIQUE N. ADAMS

Global manufacturing executive with a proven track record of leading teams to deliver transformative results. Rigorous, data-driven approach to tackling business challenges ranging from implementation of lean manufacturing principles to development and deployment of cutting-edge technologies. Strong communicator adept at navigating matrixed organizations. Talented at translating complex scientific insights into actionable policies.

Professional Experience:

Alcoa, Inc.   1998-present

Director of Global Smelting Technology Development, Knoxville, TN, U.S.A.   2012-present

Develop and execute the technology strategy for Alcoa's aluminum smelting operations. Maintain a robust pipeline of novel solutions supporting the goals of the business. Ensure safe and rapid commercialization of innovations and provide technical support across a global manufacturing footprint. Manage $12MM annual budget and an interdisciplinary team of 30 technologists located globally.

- Achieved 150% increase in annual bottom-line productivity from technology (to $35MM/yr EBITDA) by improving resource management and customer relationships.
- Grew the value of the portfolio by 50% to $600MM by restructuring the R&D management process and leveraging partnerships.
- Secured over $60MM in capital from executive leadership for project implementation despite a financial downturn.
- Achieved $12MM in new revenue through technology licensing.
- Obtained $10MM in grants over 10 years through external innovation partnerships with international universities and governments.
- Received promotions in 2013 and 2015 which led to the expansion of responsibilities, team, and budget.
- Achieved zero injuries for all staff through rigorous execution of safety programs.

Director of Global Smelting Raw Materials, Knoxville, TN, U.S.A.   2011-2012

Develop and execute the strategy for cost reduction, continuous improvement, and R&D for smelting raw materials. Provide on-site technical support to 16 smelters worldwide. Manage $1.5MM budget and team of 5 engineers in the U.S.A.

- Delivered $16MM in productivity improvements through deployment of operational best practices and technology.
- Contributed to $38MM in cost reductions by partnering with procurement, streamlining the raw material qualification process, and overseeing integration into the operations.

Manager of Carbon Materials R&D, Knoxville, TN, U.S.A.   2010-2011

Manage a global R&D portfolio related to electrode manufacturing. Manage $1MM budget and team of 3 engineers in the U.S.A.

- Delivered $3.2MM in improvements through identification and deployment of alternative electrode materials.
- Reduced time to qualify new petroleum coke suppliers by 90% by transforming the selection and utilization protocols.
- Awarded $0.2MM grant with Laval University in Quebec resulting in sponsorship of 4 students, publication of 6 papers, and hiring of one graduate.

Smelting Process Specialist, Alcoa, TN, U.S.A.   2006-2010

Deploy lean manufacturing principles at Tennessee Operations aluminum smelter to reduce variability in operational performance.

- Implemented plant-wide process monitoring system by developing the analytical tool and leading reviews with management.
- Identified critical process bottleneck which led to justification for $50MM capital expenditure to correct.
- Led a 3-person investigation of the root cause of a catastrophic failure of critical environmental processing equipment.

Senior Research and Development Engineer, Alcoa Center, PA, U.S.A.   1998-2005

Provide technical support to R&D and to operations on carbon materials properties and utilization.

- Conducted on-site due diligence assessments of potential carbon raw materials suppliers in the U.S.A. and China.
- Represented Alcoa on Executive Council of university-corporate consortium on using coal as a carbon material in manufacturing.

Education:

M.I.T., Sloan School of Management, M.B.A.	2018
Penn State, College of Earth and Mineral Sciences, Ph.D., Fuel Science	2004
Penn State, College of Earth and Mineral Sciences, M.S., Fuel Science	2002
Penn State, College of Engineering, B.S., Chemical Engineering	1997

Activities:

Member of the Corporate Board of Directors,

The Boys and Girls Clubs of the Tennessee Valley, TN, U.S.A.   2014-present

Led engagement with University of Tennessee College of Business to develop a Volunteer Management program, and obtained board sponsorship to deploy. Program achieved 1000% increase in number of volunteers and $60K in corporate grants in 12 months.

Member of The Aluminum Committee,
The Minerals, Metals, and Materials Society (TMS)   2015-present

Provide direction on technical and administrative activities for the committee.

Awards:

Sloan Leadership Fellowship, Massachusetts Institute of Technology.   2016

For demonstrating extraordinary potential in areas that add diversity to the Executive MBA program.

Alcoa Chief Information Officer Award—Productivity Category.   2016

For designing and implementing an apparatus for in-line resistivity measurement of green anodes that reduces the time required to receive quality control information from 30 days to 3 minutes.

Alcoa Impact Award—Environment, Health, and Safety Category.   2016

For developing a zero-CAPEX solution for reducing greenhouse gas emissions while improving smelter productivity through innovations in process control algorithms.

Alcoa Impact Award—Productivity Category.   2016

For implementing innovations in pot design and automation that enabled the Deschambault smelter to achieve record production.

Alcoa Impact Award—Environment, Health, and Safety Category.   2015

For developing and demonstrating on a commercial scale, a new technology to reduce SO_2 emissions from aluminum smelters, petroleum coke calciners, and waste heat boilers, at significantly lower CAPEX and OPEX then previously available on the market.

Best Paper, Alcoa Technical Center Chapter of Sigma Xi.   2015

For HORIZONTAL IN-DUCT SCRUBBING OF SULFUR-DIOXIDE FROM FLUE GAS EXHAUSTS by Rajat Ghosh, John Smith, and Angelique Adams.

Quebec Commission Santé Sécurité Travail,   **2015**
2nd place—Big Enterprise Innovation Category.

For developing a laser guided system for placement of electrodes in smelting cells which removes risks and improve workers' health and safety.

Rising Star, STEMconnector.org   **2014**

Named as a one of six Rising Stars and profiled in their 2014 publication: 100 Diverse Corporate Leaders in STEM.

Publications:

1. Ghosh, R. S., Smith, J. R., and Adams, A. (2015) *Horizontal In-Duct Scrubbing of Sulfur-Dioxide from Flue Gas Exhausts*, in Light Metals 2015 (ed. M. Hyland), John Wiley & Sons, Inc., Hoboken, NJ, USA. doi: 10.1002/9781119093435.ch99
2. Azari K., Alamdari H., Aryanpour G., Picard D., Fafard M. & Adams A., 2013. « Mixing variables for prebaked anodes used in aluminum production ». Powder Technology, vol. 235:341-348 http://dx.doi.org/10.1016/j.powtec.2012.10.043
3. Adams, A., Cahill, R., Belzile, Y., and Gendron, M., *Minimizing the Impact of Low Sulfur Coke on Anode Quality*, Essential Readings in Light Metals, Electrode Technology for Aluminum Production, John Wiley & Sons, Inc., Hoboken, NJ, USA. pp 142-147, 2013
4. Azari K., Alamdari H., Ammar H., Fafard M., Adams A. & Ziegler D., 2012, « Influence of Mixing Parameters on the Density and Compaction Behavior of Carbon, Anodes Used in Aluminum Production ». Advanced Materials Research, vol 409, pp 17-22 (doi:10.4028/www.scientific.net/AMR.409.17).
5. Adams, A.N., Schobert, H.H., Characterization of the surface properties of anode raw materials. Light Metals 2004, pp 495-498
6. Adams, A.N., Mathews, J.P., and Schobert, H.H., The use of image analysis for the optimization of pre-baked anode formulation. Light Metals 2002, pp 547-552
7. Adams, A.N., Karacan, O., Grader, A., Mathews, J.P., Halleck, P.M., and Schobert, H. H., The non-destructive 3-D characterization of pre-baked carbon anodes using X-ray computerized tomography. Light Metals 2002, pp 535-539

If you follow the interviewing guidance at manager-tools.com,[48] you will have a head start. You have already analyzed the job description and know which of your accomplishments match from Exercise 13, and you have been practicing confidently talking about your accomplishments in Exercise 6. You should now feel prepared and ready to take the next step in your career.

WHAT TO DO IF YOU ARE NOT ACTIVELY SEEKING A NEW OPPORTUNITY

This is a great position to be in because it gives you some time to get your house in order. But you should not just ignore the advice in the last two sections. You never know when the perfect opportunity will present itself, and you need to be ready. Follow the instructions I have listed above about developing and updating your LinkedIn profile and resume.

You should also consider testing the market. Let LinkedIn recruiters know you are open to opportunities. You don't have to commit to anything. But what that does is it puts you on the radar screen for recruiters, and they will start to send you messages about jobs. Use those messages as feedback. Are they the kinds of roles you are interested in? Are they at the right level of the organization? If they are, great. Keep doing what you are doing. If they aren't, then you might want to make some adjustments to your profile to emphasize different accomplishments.

Here's how to do it.

In your LinkedIn profile, you will see a box just under your name and location that indicates you can show recruiters that you are open to work. Click on "Get Started." From there, you can select the types of jobs and location you are interested in.

Show recruiters you're open to work — you control who sees this
Get started

    ✕

At the bottom of the screen, you will have an option to choose who can see that you are open to work.

Choose who sees you're open°
You decide if you want only recruiters or all LinkedIn members to see this

Select "Recruiters Only."

Let's discuss two common reservations to this approach. One is the concern about people finding out that you are open to new opportunities. You are correct, there is a risk; but in my opinion, it's small. Make sure that you put "open to work" for recruiters only, and it won't be broadcast on your profile. Only recruiters will be able to see it. They have a vested interest in maintaining confidentiality.

The second reservation is that you might be wasting recruiters' time or doing something unethical. It's not the case. It's the job of the recruiter to identify possible candidates. And you really can't say that if the job turns out to be a great opportunity, you won't become more interested than you are today. I encourage you to take their phone call if they want to talk with you. You can ask them what about your profile stood out to them. That will be useful information for you.

You are doing nothing unethical by talking with recruiters and even interviewing for a position to see what the fit is. Do not accept a position if you have no intention of actually taking it; that would be unethical. But short of that, you can engage with recruiters and hiring managers as a way of collecting data on your prospects for roles.

RECAP

After you have found potential job opportunities, you need to follow through with trying to get the positions. If your Role Fit Index is ready-now or almost ready, get your LinkedIn profile and resume ready and apply. If your Role Fit Index indicates that you have development gaps to close, make a development plan and execute it. Even if you aren't actively looking, you should get your profile and resume up to date so that when the opportunities do come your way, you can seize them immediately.

THE FOURTH KEY:

HOW TO TAKE ON MORE WITHOUT BEING OVERWHELMED

CHAPTER 7

THE SECRET TO TAKING ON NEW PROJECTS AND GETTING AMAZING RESULTS QUICKLY

"What is holding me back from my next career goal? That's easy, time."

—Brenda

In this chapter, you will learn:

1. Why most people don't take on new projects, and why you should.
2. How a common technique from the manufacturing industry can help you excel in your career.
3. The other way to beat overwhelm—asking for help.

WHY MOST PEOPLE DON'T TAKE ON NEW PROJECTS, AND WHY YOU SHOULD

According to the Mercer report,[37] 87 percent of employees experience barriers to learning new skills, and the most commonly cited issue is time. On the other hand, if you want a new job, there is no way around it—you will have to learn new skills and take on new responsibilities. As we discussed in Chapter 6, for your ready-later roles, you will be taking on learn-by-doing projects for a development plan. For your ready-now roles, you might be doing similar work but in a different context, for example, in a new department or a completely new organization. Or you might be doing completely different projects that will require you to overcome a learning curve.

What! How will I find the time!

When you take on new challenges, it can be completely overwhelming to figure out what to do. You have thousands of thoughts swirling through your mind. You get worried about not knowing things. You stare at a blank piece of paper or blank screen and think, *I am never going to figure this out*, or, *How am I going to find the time to figure this out?* And you imagine that you have to do it all by yourself. With all those challenges running through your mind, it's no wonder that you talk yourself out of taking on anything new.

What if I told you there was a magic formula that you could use to approach any new project quickly and effectively, even if you don't know the subject matter?

Recently, I agreed to do some pro bono strategy consulting for a local nonprofit that focuses on academic achievement and confidence building for girls ages five to fourteen. A very worthy cause . . . that I knew nothing about. I scheduled a one-hour introduction session with the executive director, whom I hadn't met yet. As she was telling me about her situation, I was furiously taking notes. At the end, I summarized what I heard: this is your current situation, this is what you wish the situation was, here is what you think the reasons are for this problem, and here is how you think I might be able to help. Then I asked, "Did I get that right?" She said, "Wow, that is an excellent synopsis. I can't believe you got that out of my twenty minutes of rambling. You are spot on. Yes that is what I want to do; can you help me?"

How was I able to transform a rambling mess of ideas on a topic I knew nothing about into a clearly communicated summary and action plan in an hour?

Easy, the A3+5Y formula.

Okay, so what am I talking about? I am going to give you a brief introduction, go through the methodology, and show you several examples.

A COMMON MANUFACTURING TECHNIQUE CAN HELP YOU CONQUER OVERWHELM AT WORK

A3 and 5Y refer to two problem-solving methodologies that have been used for decades by the manufacturing sector as part of the Toyota Production System (TPS).[49, 50, 51] I have used the methodologies for over twenty years to solve problems ranging from losing five million dollars on a failed product launch to not having enough donations for a local nonprofit.

A NOTE TO TPS EXPERTS. *I've oversimplified important tools in the TPS system. Remember, my goal here is give women a template to quickly organize their thoughts and actions around a problem, not become experts. I encourage you to be open-minded and try using the simplified version on problems that are outside of your day-to-day work. You might find, as I have, that when you free yourself from the rules associated with these methodologies, you find broad applicability.*

Introduction to the A3[52]

It's called an A3 because the report was originally written on one single sheet of A3 paper (297 x 420 mm or approximately 11 x 17 in). Don't worry, you can use whatever paper you have. Note: throughout this chapter, I will be using A3s from my personal files to illustrate the methodology. Here is an example of a completed A3.

Figure 33. Example A3 #1

A3: Training Example

Problem Statement

Staff not adequately completing tasks ask design resulting in organization not meeting production goals

Current Condition

Classroom training → In-field training → Certification test → Ongoing coaching and feedback / Performance Management auditing

Benchmark Pathway to Proficiency for tasks

Target Condition

Classroom training → In-field training → Certification test → Ongoing coaching and feedback / Performance Management auditing

Root Cause Analysis

1. Trainers not proficient in the material
2. Trainers are learning 2x the material in ½ the time
3. Trainers leave role before finishing curriculum
4. Trainers leave because they are frustrated with lack of feedback
5. No coaches available to provide needed feedback

Action Plan/Next Steps

Action	SPA	By When
Increase training duration to meet benchmarks	K. Smith	14 days
Benchmark other locations for coaching program	K. Smith	30 days
Implement coaching program	K. Smith	45 days

Results

Action	Result
Implement coaching program	Trainer turnover reduced by 50%

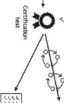

Figure 34. Example A3 #2

A3: New Product Example

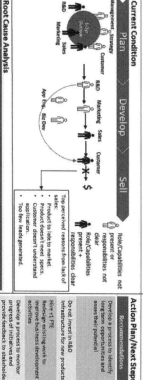

Problem Statement

Globe Corp invested $3MM to develop new products and have achieved $0 in sales vs a target of $1.5MM. Globe Corp is spending $1.5MM/yr. to maintain R&D and sales staff to support the existing portfolio with no clear plan for improving sales performance or conducting future development work.

Current Condition

Plan → Develop → Sell

- Role/Capabilities not present or responsibilities not clear
- Role/Capabilities present + responsibilities clear

Top perceived reasons from lack of sales:
- Product is late to market.
- Product doesn't meet specs.
- Customer doesn't understand application.
- Too few leads generated.

Root Cause Analysis — Summary of 20 potential Why trees

Process Step	
Plan	Strategic planning process doesn't reach internal 1-3 yr. marketing plans or 3-5 yr. development plan
Plan	No clear process for getting customer input (e.g., advisory board)
Develop	Inadequate R&D practices to conduct stage of performance testing required by customers
Sell	No go-to-market strategy for new products
Sell	No clear feedback process for updating strategy

Target Condition

Plan → Develop → Sell

Strategy	Investment	Potential Benefits
Abandon	0	$-3M
Empty Pipeline	$1.5M/yr.	$5M/yr.
Evergreen pipeline	$10MM CAPEX	TBD

Action Plan/Next Steps

Recommendations	Rationale	SPA/By When
Do not invest in R&D infrastructure for new products.	Repurpose R&D FTE to other development projects	F. Jones to outline new products (+ 30 days)
Develop a process to identify long-term opportunities and asses their potential	Need is independent of product development. Value creation activities. Technology portfolio development	Commercial framework complete. Detailed technical framework (+ 60 days upon approval/A. Adams)
Hire +1 FTE. Redesign existing work to improve business development activities	Exploit traction we have with customers. FTE will also close success plan gaps	F. Jones to post position (+30 days). M. Moore (+ 30 days upon approval)
Develop a process to monitor progress of initiatives and provide feedback to stakeholders	Ensure stakeholder alignment and rapid learning in new commercial environments	M. Moore (+ 30 days pending decision)

Results

Action	Result
Hire	New R&D staff hired
Feedback process	2 customers agreed to test product

Here are the components of an A3 (overview):

1. Problem Statement: What problem are we trying to solve?

2. Current Condition (CC): What is actually going on right now?

3. Root Cause Analysis (A): Why is the problem occurring?

4. Target Condition (TC): What will it be like if the problem went away?

5. Action Plan/Next Steps (NS): How will we fix it?

6. Results and Lessons Learned (R): What have we learned that we can apply elsewhere?

EXERCISE 15: BUILDING AN A3

You will need your workbook or two sheets of paper. On one sheet of paper, create the following table.

Figure 35. A3 Template

A3: PROBLEM NAME	
Problem Statement	Target Condition
Current Condition	Action Plan
Root Cause Analysis	Results and Lessons Learned

STEP 1: BRAIN DUMP.

On the other sheet of paper, write down all the information you have or the questions that you have about the problem you are trying to solve.

STEP 2: DRAFT THE INFORMATION THAT YOU HAVE INTO THE APPROPRIATE SECTIONS.

Use the guiding questions below to help you place what you have in the right boxes.

PRO TIP: Expect lots of blank spaces, especially if this is a new project.

- Problem Statement: What problem are we trying to solve?
    - Why is it an important problem?
    - For whom is the problem important?
    - How will you know if the problem is solved? What starts to happen? What stops happening?

PRO TIP: A good problem statement has an observable problem. This means you can see it directly or collect data about it.

- Current Condition:
    - What is actually going on right now?
    - Who are the people involved?
    - What processes are involved?
    - What are the metrics being used?

PRO TIP: Whenever you can, go and see it for yourself and talk to the people actually doing the work.

- Root Cause Analysis:
    - Why is the problem occurring?
    - Implement the 5Y (5 Whys) technique to dig deep and get to the bottom of the issue.

PRO TIP: See the next section for the 5Y root cause analysis technique.

- Target Condition:
    - What will it be like if the problem went away?
    - Who are the people involved?
    - What processes are involved?
    - What are the metrics being used?
    - What will be the new targets for those metrics?
- Action Plan:
    - How will we fix it?
    - Who does what, and by when? (Name of person, action, due date.)

PRO TIP: Never write an action plan without all three pieces of information—name of person, action, due date—and an agreement from the parties involved. And who will be involved always refers to a person with a face, name, and email address. If you leave it at the department level, you will be chasing people around. If you can't identify the person to do the job, put in the action plan the name of the person who is going to identify the person.

- Results and Lessons Learned:
    - What have we learned that we can apply elsewhere?

STEP 3: IDENTIFY YOUR RESOURCES AND GET INPUT.

Figure out how to get the information you need.

- Can you ask someone to help you?
- Can you find the appropriate sources in the literature?
- Can you go and check the situation yourself?

STEP 4: GATHER INFORMATION.

PRO TIP: When you are interviewing stakeholders, don't worry about where the information goes. Just capture the inputs and organize the information later.

STEP 5: SHARE AND GET FEEDBACK.

This is a living document. Be prepared to update it regularly as you get new information.

An introduction to the 5Y Technique

The 5Y technique, also called the 5 Whys, is a root cause analysis method.[53] It's designed to get through surface reasons to the real cause of any problem. To use the technique, you simply write down the problem statement and ask why it is occurring. Ask the same question "Why?" five times, and the last answer is the root cause. The way to solve the problem is to find a solution to the root cause. Below is an example.[54]

Figure 36. 5Y Example

PROBLEM STATEMENT:	OUR CLIENT IS REFUSING TO PAY FOR LEAFLETS WE PRINTED.
Why?	The delivery was late, so the leaflets couldn't be used.
Why?	The job took longer than we expected.
Why?	We ran out of printer ink.
Why?	The ink was all consumed on a large last-minute order.
Why?	We didn't have enough ink in stock and couldn't order new supplies in time.
Possible Solution:	Find an ink supplier who can deliver on short notice

EXERCISE 16: CONDUCTING A 5Y ANALYSIS

You will need your workbook or one sheet of paper. Label the page "5Ys Exercise."

It should look like this:

Figure 37. 5Y Template

PROBLEM STATEMENT:	
Why?	
Why?	
Why?	
Why?	
Why?	
Possible Solution:	

STEP 1: WRITE DOWN YOUR PROBLEM STATEMENT.

STEP 2: ASK WHY THE PROBLEM IS OCCURRING, AND WRITE DOWN THE ANSWER.

STEP 3: REPEAT THE PROCESS UNTIL YOU HAVE ASKED WHY FIVE TIMES.

Note: For complex problems, it's likely that you will find more than one possible why. In those cases, you will have a tree of potential causes to evaluate. The diagram below shows an example.

Figure 38: Example of 5Y with multiple causes

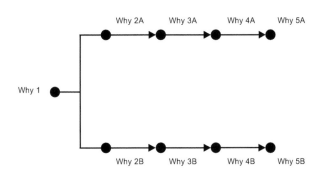

Now you have the templates and methodologies. But how does this process actually help you become less overwhelmed? There are four ways this formula can help you handle the problems at hand and take on more.

1. CONQUERS THE FEAR OF THE BLANK PAGE. By having a go-to template for organizing ideas, you will always have a place to start.

2. PROVIDES A STRUCTURED AND REPEATABLE WAY TO SOLVE COMPLEX PROBLEMS. The 5Y methodology is a proven approach. Once you get more practice with it, you will have a consistent way to solve problems.

3. CREATES A BUILT-IN COMMUNICATION STRUCTURE. As you might have noticed, the A3 template uses the same Key Project Elements discussed in Chapter 4. As a result, it has a built-in communication plan. You simply need to analyze your audience and context and determine the appropriate language to use.

4. HELPS YOU IDENTIFY WHERE TO ENLIST HELP TO COMPLETE YOUR INITIATIVES.
    Through the process of collecting the information to
    complete the A3 and using it as a communication tool,
    you will be engaging with others. As you do so, you can
    identify stakeholders who have the resources to help
    you with your project.

THE OTHER WAY TO CONQUER OVERWHELM—ASKING FOR HELP

> "I was worried I would lose my career entirely.
> But my employer compromised with me, and I work part time now.
> It is exactly what I needed."
>
> —LYDIA

As I discussed earlier in this section, the A3 makes it easier
to enlist help with your project. You can easily communicate
the key elements and identify where you have gaps that
need to be filled in. But what about when we aren't talking
about projects at all? What if you are struggling at work
because you have an issue at home? What do you do then?

The most difficult lesson I have learned in my career is
that it's okay to ask your boss for help on nonwork-related
issues. There is not a clear separation between work and
home life. In my first year as a leader, one of my direct

reports lost his home in a fire and another of my direct reports needed to take a leave of absence in order to care for a family member with a mental illness. While I was not exactly sure how best to handle each situation, I was certain that, as their boss, it was my role to do my best to utilize the resources I had to help them. I didn't question it.

Yet I have been reluctant to see if I would be afforded the same benefits myself. It hasn't been until just recently that I felt like I could sit down with my boss to discuss a scheduling issue that was a challenge for me. Of course, he was eager to help me find a solution—good bosses want to work with their employees.

As Jack Welch noted in his bestselling book *Winning*, "Most bosses are perfectly willing to accommodate work-life balance challenges if you have earned it with performance." [55] With that in mind, there are two questions you need to answer:

1. Have I earned the right to ask for help?
2. How do I ask for help?

To answer question one, I refer you to your own list of accomplishments. Review Exercise 1 and Exercise 2 from Chapter 1. Have you demonstrated that you are a good employee worthy of support? I am confident that you have.

For question two, you need to recognize that while your organization wants to help you, there are rules associated with providing additional or different resources. So, you need to demonstrate that you are sensitive to the constraints and be ready to address them with the people you are asking for help.

Here is a checklist of homework I suggest you do before asking your organization to help you manage nonwork-related items.

CHECKLIST 3: ASKING FOR HELP WITH NONWORK-RELATED ISSUES

- Is what you are asking for addressed in the employee manual or other human resources policy? If yes, be prepared to highlight the relevant policy and indicate that what you are asking for is consistent or not with the policy.
- Does what you are asking for require spending money?
- What is the duration of the help required?
- What will you be able to do to help your organization if you receive the help?

RECAP

If you want to continue to grow in your career, you will need to take on more tasks. Most people avoid doing that because they don't want to devote the time and effort to do so. You can differentiate yourself by being willing to take on more. The A3+5Y framework is a well-tested tool to organize your thoughts, define the key elements of your project, and help you identify where you can enlist colleagues to help you tackle the challenges. Furthermore, the framework is aligned with the STEM Insights Communication Framework you learned in Chapter 4, thus reducing the time you need to prepare for status updates and report outs. Finally, as you continue to achieve at work, know that it's okay to ask for help when you need it. You've earned it.

THE FIFTH KEY:

5

HOW TO HANDLE
THE HATERS

CHAPTER 8

WHY SMART, TALENTED TRAILBLAZERS FEEL CRITICIZED AND JUDGED

"There are people in this world—friends, family, or other colleagues in your workplace— who will tell you sometimes directly or with subtle messaging that you are not ready for the next career move."

—SATYA

In this chapter, you will learn:

1. Why you are easy prey for critics.
2. How to decide what is really important.
3. How to take away the power of critics.

Before I start this chapter, let me define what I mean by haters. I am referring to people who make negative comments about you, typically about your choices. These can be your personal choices, such as how you spend your time or how you spend your money. They can be your professional choices, such as what you choose to do for work or how you execute your tasks. These people probably have some of the characteristics you noted in Exercise 4: The Enjoy/Dread List. In general, these people display behaviors that occur within the range of "acceptable" but are causing problems for you personally.

I am not talking about people who threaten you with violence, intimidation, or humiliation. If you feel threatened, you can seek help through your local human resources department or law enforcement department.

WHY YOU ARE EASY PREY FOR CRITICS

> "I wish my colleagues knew how guilt rules my life so that I say yes to things and feel bad about missing out."
>
> —ANGELA

We all have demands on our time: Family and friends who need us, a hobby that we are passionate about, and a side-hustle that we dream will one day allow us to live that coveted four-hour workweek.[56] Even if you don't have and never plan to have children, there is too much to do and not enough time to do it. As a result, you are constantly making choices about what you prioritize in your life. As with all choices in life, not everyone will agree with what you decide. People will comment and criticize.

To make matters worse, we are constantly getting the message that no matter what we choose, when it comes to our career, we have failed. In comes the notion of "having it all." It might be the most controversial topic in this book and maybe the most controversial topic for women in the workplace. At the time of this writing, there are over eight thousand books on "work-life balance" on Amazon.com and over one million blog posts on the topic. Most of what is written falls into two categories:

Category 1: Give up.

What you need to be successful is either outside of your control or not readily changeable.[57] Examples of this category are discussions about the lack of access to childcare, lack of access to long-term care for aging families, workplace wage disparities, and inequitable distribution of labor in the home. In other words, you can't have it all until society fixes childcare and health care, and you fix your partner.

Category 2: Try harder.58

If you are clever and try really, really hard, you don't have to choose—you can do everything. Examples in this category are discussions about eliminating fun stuff (TV, social media)[59] and combining tasks.[60] In other words, productivity hacks.

Don't be fooled by what I call the "rename fakeout." These are the comments and advice that say, "It isn't balancing, its *juggling*,"[61] or "It isn't balancing, it is _____ _____." These just reframe the same problem with a clever metaphor.

Whether you give up and feel defeated or try harder and feel defeated, this dichotomy is a lose-lose proposition. When you are already feeling low, any negative comments from people (even people you don't really care about) are amplified. As a result, you feel guilty and judged. This is why you are easy prey for haters.

I have experienced this firsthand many times. When I had my first child, I took work-life balance literally. Before I returned to work, I made a spreadsheet of the hours in the day in thirty-minute increments. I blocked out time I would be with my son and time I would be away from him. In my mind, if at the end of a week I was spending more time with him, even just thirty minutes more, I was a good mother. I would have achieved work-life balance.

I diligently kept this log for weeks. It became harder and harder to achieve the "balance." As the weeks passed, work ramped up and I needed to stay at the office later. At the same time, my son started to go to bed earlier and sleep through the night. There were fewer and fewer "with Seth" boxes being checked on my spreadsheet.

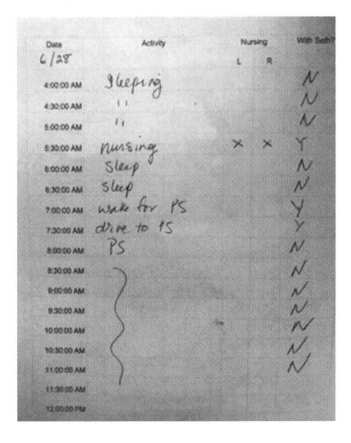

Then I went on my first business trip. As I was having dinner with my colleagues and their spouses, one wife said to me, "Wow, you have a baby. I wouldn't leave my dog alone with my husband overnight, let alone my child!"

Chastened, I redoubled my efforts to spend more time with Seth. This kind of measuring led me to the morning when my husband found me in our son's room asleep on the floor, my back against his crib. I was trying desperately to get the few more minutes "with Seth" (touching the crib counts, doesn't it?) that I needed for my spreadsheet to balance so I would be a "good mother."

When I told my husband what I was doing, he gently but firmly told me that I was misguided. "Do you see how Seth's face lights up every time you walk into the room? Why don't you consider that? See how happy he is? See how much he is growing and exceeding all his milestones? You are a great mom!"

I had spent so much time trying not to make a tradeoff that I wasn't enjoying the time I had with Seth and I wasn't paying attention to the signs about whether or not my actions were even getting the desired result.

HOW TO DECIDE WHAT IS REALLY IMPORTANT TO YOU

What I learned at that low point was that I had to find a way to be okay with the choices I make about how I prioritize my time. Rather than fall into the trap of giving up or trying harder, I had to accept that I have to make tradeoffs. I had to accept my decisions. If you are confident in the choices you make, you will eliminate the guilt and be resilient to critics.

Managing your life without the guilt is possible. I am living proof.

I have a happy marriage with two healthy, active tweens who still like to have family game nights. I am healthy and active myself. I am an executive at a multibillion-dollar firm. I do pro bono strategy consulting, and I am side hustling with this book. Actually, I am more like side crawling right now, but nevertheless you get the point.

Are you rolling your eyes yet?

If you are anything like me, you are reading this with skepticism. I know that when I used to meet a woman who seemed successful, my first thought was always, *What is the catch?* There must be some reason she can succeed and I can't. She's been divorced several times. She doesn't take care of her health. She doesn't have any kids. She has kids but they hate her. Her partner stays at home. She is rich and throws money at her problems.

None of those things are true for me. But I have made tradeoffs. I travel a lot and have missed birthday parties and piano recitals. My circle of friends is quite small.

I am okay with all those things. You might think I am selfish, a bad mother, a bad partner, etc. That is the point. I am okay with the tradeoffs that I am making in my life, and I am okay with the fact that you might disagree. This is where you want to be: internally confident and externally resilient.

How did I get here? I need to be honest—this didn't happen overnight. I have been working on it for years.

But it's possible. I have found success with a two-pronged approach. First, you must decide what is most important to you; and second, you have to take action toward your goals, monitor the results, and make sure they are having the desired impact.

How to get clarity on what is important to you

The Perfect Day Story is a visioning exercise that will help you get crystal clear on what is important to you.

EXERCISE 17: YOUR PERFECT DAY STORY

Using your workbook or a blank sheet of paper, put the following headings for your Perfect Day Story outline: "Setting," "Characters," and "Plot." It should look like this.

Figure 39. Your Perfect Day Story Template

IN MY PERFECT DAY, I AM ...	DESCRIPTIONS
Setting	
Characters	
Plot	

STEP 1. USE THE GUIDING QUESTIONS BELOW TO FILL IN YOUR OUTLINE.

Setting

- Describe your physical location.
- Where is your home?
- Where is your work?

Characters

- Who is in your life?
- Who do you spend your mornings with and your evenings with?
- Who do you work with? What do you like most about working with them?
- Describe your friends. What do you like most about them?
- Whose lives do you impact?

- Who do you help? Who helps you?

Plot

- What is your daily schedule?
- What do you do for work?
- What do you do for leisure?
- How are you impacting the lives of your characters? How are they impacting you?

NOTE: Save your outline. You are going to use it in a later exercise.

STEP 2. WRITE THE STORY.

- I suggest you leave the outline for a few days and come back to it.
- When you are ready, write a story about your perfect day.
- The power is in the details.
- Make them vivid so you can actually see the day happening in your mind.
- If you are like me and don't know where to start, you can describe your day in chronological order.

Now you have your Perfect Day Story. This perfect day describes in one twenty-four-hour period what you consider to be most important in your life. Are you already living your perfect day? Probably not. If you were, you wouldn't have picked up this book. But you can get there.

How to take action toward what is most important to you

The next part of the approach is to start to take actions to get you closer to what is most important to you. What actions should you take?

Before you can answer that, you need to understand why you chose the elements in your Perfect Day Story in the first place. By understanding the why, you will have even more clarity and therefore even more certainty about what is important to you.[62]Let's use your Perfect Day Story and the root cause analysis methodology we learned in Chapter 7 to dig a little bit deeper.

EXERCISE 18: IDENTIFYING WHY YOUR PERFECT DAY IS IMPORTANT TO YOU

You will need your Perfect Day Story outline from Exercise 16, and you will need to create a 5Y table like you did in Exercise 15.

STEP 1. SELECT ONE KEY POINT FROM YOUR STORY.

Follow the 5Y methodology from Exercise 15 to really understand why this point is important to you. I've changed the headings slightly to fit the new topic. It should look like this:

Figure 40. 5Y Analysis for Your Perfect Day Template

PERFECT DAY STORY ELEMENT	
1. Why is this important to me?	
2. Why?	
3. Why?	
4. Why?	
5. Why?	
Core Life Theme:	

I recommend that you repeat this exercise for at least one element in each of your Setting, Characters, and Plot categories.

Here is an example of a 5Y analysis from my own Perfect Day Story.

Figure 41. 5Y Analysis for Your Perfect Day Example

PERFECT DAY STORY ELEMENT	PLOT: "I WAKE UP EARLY AND WORK OUT."
1. Why is this important to me?	I know that when I wake up early, I work out consistently.
2. Why?	I want to be fit.
3. Why?	I want to look and feel good.
4. Why?	I want to be in good health.
5. Why?	I don't want to have to take a lot of medications when I get older.
Core Life Theme:	Healthy body

After you have done your 5Y's analysis you will be left with a few core life themes; these are the ideas that are at the heart of what you believe is needed to have the life of your dreams. Now that you have identified what they are, you can put a plan together and go after them. Here are some of my favorite resources for identifying actions that support your Perfect Day core life themes.

Figure 42. Resources for Exploring Your Perfect Day Core Life Themes

IF YOUR CORE THEMES ARE ABOUT	RESOURCES I HAVE PERSONALLY USED
Building strong relationships	The Five Love Languages (website)[63] *Grace-Based Parenting* (book)[64]
Improving your physical and mental health	Precision Nutrition (blog)[65] Darebee (blog)[66] *Why We Sleep* (book)[67]
Increasing your financial wealth	*The Index Card* (book)[68] *The 9 Steps to Financial Freedom* (book)[69]
Helping others	*The Generosity Factor* (book)[70]
Learning new things	Coursera (online courses)[71]
Being creative	*The Artist's Way* (book)[72]

It's quite possible that the themes and resources that I list above don't resonate with you. That is okay. If you need more inspiration to help you uncover the core themes in your own life, I recommend you conduct a character strengths assessment.[73] This online tool (free at the time of this writing) is a science-based survey to help you uncover the fundamental nature of your personality based on twenty-four character traits. You can find it at https://www.viacharacter.org. Once you identify which of those traits most resonate with you, you can use the same resource to identify actions you can take to reinforce the traits that are important to you.

EXERCISE 19: ACTING ON YOUR PERFECT DAY CORE LIFE THEMES

Using your workbook or a blank sheet of paper, put the following headings for your Perfect Day Action Plan: "Core Theme," "Action Plan," and "Review Comments". It should look like this.

PERFECT DAY CORE THEME	ACTON PLAN	REVIEW COMMENTS
	This week I will 1 2 3	
	This month I will 1 2 3	
	In the next 6 months I will 1 2 3	

STEP 1: IDENTIFY ONE OF YOUR PERFECT DAY THEMES.

STEP 2: RESEARCH ACTIONS THAT SUPPORT YOUR THEME.

Brainstorm all the potential actions you can take to achieve your goal. The longer the list, the more the opportunities you have to succeed.

STEP 3: DEVELOP AN ACTION PLAN.

Develop an action plan along three time horizons.

- What will I do in the next week?
- What will I do in the next month?
- What will I do in the next six months?

STEP 4: REVIEW THE ACTION PLAN AND ADJUST.

Review your plan on a weekly basis. Are you making progress? How does it feel? Do you need to try something different? If you do, revisit your list and select a new set of actions.

HOW TO TAKE AWAY THE POWER OF CRITICS

In the same way that I recommended that you remind yourself about the accomplishments you have achieved on a regular basis, I also recommend that you remind yourself about what is important to you on a regular basis. Just as we use repetition to push out self-doubt about our skills, we are going to use repetition to push out self-doubt about our decisions. In doing so, we can boost our resilience against critics.

You need to focus for a few brief moments every day to remind yourself of what you care about. There are many ways to do this. I suggest you use trial and error to find whatever method you enjoy enough to make a lifelong habit. Here are a few ideas:

Figure 43: Approaches and Resources for Daily Reminders

IF YOU LIKE	YOU CAN TRY
Visuals	Making a vision board[74]
Listening	Reciting affirmations or prayers[75]
Writing	Journaling[76]

I write down my Perfect Day Core Life Themes on a scrap piece of paper or a 3x5 note card every day.

Here they are:

Figure 44: Example of Daily Reminders of Perfect Day Core Life Themes

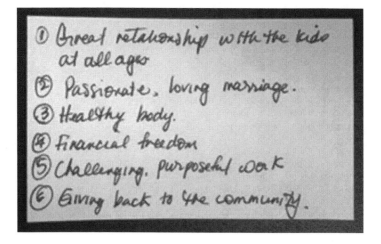

EXERCISE 20: DAILY REMINDER OF WHAT I CARE ABOUT MOST

STEP 1: SELECT A METHOD TO CREATE A REMINDER OF WHAT IS IMPORTANT TO YOU.

STEP 2: COMPLETE THE METHOD.

STEP 3: REVIEW IT DAILY

RECAP

Haters are people who criticize you for the choices you make. The best way to take their power away is to own your choices. Get clarity on what is truly important to you and act in accordance with your strategy. Develop an action plan, implement it, and review it regularly to ensure that it's moving you in the right direction. Remind yourself on a regular basis why you are on the path you are on.

PUTTING IT ALL TOGETHER

CHAPTER 9

HOW TO KEEP GOING

"I linked my happiness only to my Efforts. After giving my best efforts, I accepted whatever results came. Then everything worked out magically!"

—PRABHA

In this chapter, you will learn:

1. How to put all the pieces together with the You're More Than a Diversity Hire®
2. Quick Reference Guide.
3. How to effectively change the system.
4. What to do next.

HOW TO USE THE TOOLS IN THE BOOK ON AN ONGOING BASIS

In this book, you have learned the five keys to unlocking your true potential:

1. How to tell if you are truly good enough to reach your goals.
2. How to claim your voice and command respect, with scripts for important conversations, meetings, and interviews.
3. How to stop waiting for your manager and HR and develop a career roadmap that YOU control.
4. How to take on new challenges at work and still have time for what you care about with the A3+5Y formula.
5. How to handle the haters and what to do when your colleagues, friends, and family decide that you are too ambitious.

I wish I could tell you that if you go through this book one time, all your problems will be solved for good. That is not how life works. While I am confident that this book will help you overcome the challenges that are right in front of you today, I am equally confident that new challenges will arise. Fortunately, the proven methods that I have outlined here will continue to work for you throughout your career. The trick is to spot the new situation you are in and identify the right tool to address it. To help you with that, I have created a quick reference guide.

For example, if you are planning to pursue a new opportunity, you can start with Chapter 5 and work your way through it to land the job. If you need to take on a new project either as a development plan or whenever you get the new role, you can move to Chapter 7. But what if the situation isn't so obvious? What if you find yourself frustrated for a few days, or worse a few weeks, in a row, and you can't figure out why? For those instances, use this reference guide to help you identify the best tool for the situation you are in.

Figure 45: You're More Than a Diversity Hire® Quick Reference Guide

WHEN YOU . . .	DO
Doubt you are good enough.	Exercise 1: Realistic Goals Assessment
Feel like you aren't doing anything right these days.	Exercise 3: The Small Wins Inventory
Want to know if you have the skills for a new job.	Exercise 13: Job Qualifications Analysis
Want to put your best foot forward in an important meeting with peers or leaders.	Exercise 7: High-Stakes Meeting Preparation and Outcome Tracker
Want to tout your skills or experience to peers or leaders but don't want to be seen as boastful or arrogant.	Exercise 6: Bragging the Right Way
Question your choices about how you are spending your time.	Exercise 6: Bragging the Right Way

WHEN YOU . . .	DO
Question your choices about how you are spending your time.	Exercise 17: Your Perfect Day Story and Exercise 18: Identifying Why Your Perfect Day Is Important to You
Have to present your work to an important audience	Exercise 12: Creating Your Own STEM Insights BLUF
Feel overwhelmed by a new project or challenges.	Exercise 14: Building an A3
Hear hurtful comments from family, friends, or coworkers.	Exercise 19: Daily Reminder of What I Care about Most

HOW TO CHANGE THE SYSTEM

As I said in the introduction, this book has been mostly about you and giving you the tools you need to succeed in today's male-dominated STEM workplaces. That is, how to work with the system that we have. But you and I both know that the system for women in STEM is far from ideal. Only you can decide if, when, and how you want to change things. Here, I am going to suggest a few ideas to get you started.

A tip that works for any kind of change

First and foremost, remember that if you want to persuade people to do something different, you need to command respect on the topic and with the audience you are trying to influence. In other words, use the techniques you learned in Chapter 4. Analyze the audience and context. Figure out what matters to the people you are trying to convince. Use clear BLUF statements to get their attention and state your arguments.

Here are two small but high-impact ways you can change the system for women in the workplace.

Stop people from interrupting and stealing IDEAS

As we discussed in Chapter 3, you learned a way to handle the tricky situation of being interrupted. But what if you aren't the one speaking? One very simple way to promote women in the workplace is to acknowledge their contributions. Here is how it works. When a woman, in this case we will call her Gloria, says a relevant point in a meeting, immediately follow her comment with this script:

SCRIPT 7: STOPPING MEETING INTERRUPTERS, THE GOOD POINT, GLORIA, TECHNIQUE

"Good point, Gloria."

That is it.

Why does this work?

1. It's a noncontroversial phrase that is already commonly used.
2. It doesn't require you to call out or enter into a conflict with anyone.
3. It interrupts the pervasive negative experience that women have in the workplace on a regular basis: male colleagues taking credit for their ideas.

After you start to feel more confident about getting your own questions and thoughts out in work meetings, you can move to this advanced technique and start helping others. As you probably already know, some of the same forces that make workplace communications difficult for women are at play for other underrepresented groups like people of color. Consider using it for any colleague whose voice is seldom heard. And, afterward, make sure you put it on your Small Wins list.

Promote Alternative Career Progression

As I discussed in Chapter 5, the system has very outdated ideas about career progression. When you get to be in the room with the leaders discussing who gets chosen to receive resources for development and who doesn't, now is your chance to have a real impact. When you are in the room, you can advocate for people to be considered as high potential even if they don't want to be on the fast track. Here is an example of how it could work.

SCRIPT 8: PROMOTING ALTERNATIVE CAREER PROGRESSION

"I think that *insert Name* is a high-potential candidate. We've checked with her, and she isn't in a position to take on a bigger role right now, but I want to make sure she stays on our list for our next review. Here are my points supporting her designation (*insert supporting accomplishments in the format outlined in Exercise 2*)."

It's possible that you get some resistance. I have personally never seen it happen because, most of the time, nobody else bothers to bring a list of accomplishments for other nominees to this discussion. Even just two highlights that are stated well will stand out in the discussion. I recommend you be insistent.

What is more likely to happen is that everyone says, "Okay," because frankly they don't want to prolong the discussion. If you have never been in a talent review discussion, they are normally four to five hours long and sometimes quite monotonous. Your HR professional will then note the person's name down as a HiPo for the next round of discussions. When the discussions arise, you can talk about the candidate again. Or if she becomes available for a new role before that, you can remind everyone that she was designated a HiPo, and your HR professional will confirm.

You've now just made a change to the system. You have just sealed a crack that so many women fall through.

I find the simplicity of this action both refreshing and frustrating. On the one hand, it takes so little effort to make a couple of statements to promote a candidate that otherwise would have been forgotten. On the other hand, only people already in the room get to make these statements. When you are in the room, please don't squander the opportunity.

Leveraging external organizations to affect change.

There is a myriad of ways you can try to affect positive change for women in STEM. There are thousands of organizations out there doing great work in this area. I am just listing the ones I have personally interacted with.

Figure 46. Summary of Organizations Supporting Women in STEM

ORGANIZATION NAME	MISSION
Girls Inc.[77]	Inspires all girls to be strong, smart, and bold
Catalyst.org[78]	Workplaces that work for women
Society of Women Engineers[79]	The world's largest advocate for women in engineering and technology

ORGANIZATION NAME	MISSION
Listed LinkedIn Groups (Listed groups are discoverable via search. You can join by sending the administrator a request.)	
WiSER (Women in Science, Engineering, and Research)	A community of individuals with STEM backgrounds at various career levels in industry, government, and academia
Global Diversity and Inclusion in the Workplace	This group is comprised of professional business people from across the globe who discuss ways to initiate and implement diversity and inclusion principles in the organizations where they work
International Women in Mining (IWiM)	IWiM aims to lead a global change in attitudes and behaviors to achieve gender parity in mining

WHAT TO DO NEXT

Thank you very much for taking the time to read this book. I hope that by the time you have gotten here, you will know that you are not alone in your struggles and will feel confident that you have the tools to overcome them.

I have a few suggestions for what you can do next.

Join the community

As I interviewed successful women from around the world for this book, it became clear to me that we need a community. We have so much in common yet we feel alone. We need a place to talk openly and honestly about what it really takes to excel in our jobs. We need a place to celebrate our wins and a place to lift us up when we stumble. Unfortunately, we can't get that at work. So, I created the community myself. I started an exclusive LinkedIn group for women just like you. It's free and there are no sales pitches. To join, just connect with me and put in your note that you want to join the Lady Visitor Project group.

https://www.linkedin.com/in/angeliqueadams/

Connect with me

I would love to hear how the book has helped you. Please send me an email and tell me one thing you learned: angelique@drangeliqueadams.com

Spread the word

Please consider spreading the word by writing a review and telling your friends and colleagues about the book.

ACKNOWLEDGMENTS

My husband, Dr. James Szybist. His unwavering support for everything that I do is a precious gift.

My parents, Andre and Cynthia Adams, for their encouragement. My dad for being a great PR guy. My mom for using her skills as a former elementary school teacher to serve as my first developmental editor and alpha reader. She probably read this book twenty times.

MIT Executive MBA class of 2018. The women who taught me that my lowest points were my greatest strengths. The men who showed me that when I had something to say, they were listening with interest.

Cory Little, founder of Formation Consulting Group. Cory helped me to strengthen my own emotional intelligence and to see that my experience could be packaged and shared with others.

Karin Roest, founder of Purposely Famous Academy. Karin helped me discover what would resonate with my audience. She taught me that I needed to be vulnerable and open and that I could find a way to be comfortable doing it.

The Lady Visitor Project supporters. These people provided interviews, insights, referrals, and encouragement for my project.

Allison M.	Donna L.	Keirsten F.
Alon S.	Duygu K.	Kelly D.
Amy H.	Eden F.	Kim H.
Ana Maria S.	Elizabeth A.	Kristin R.
Andre A.	Emily W.	Lauren D
Andrea S.	Erin C.	Lauren B.
Angela F.	Fatima H.	Leena P.
Angela L.	Fernanda S.	Linda L.
April W.	Gayatri A.	Maggie C.
Ashley B.	Hongyu C.	Malika H.
Bart M.	Ipek S.	Manjusha I.
Brenda S.	Irene B.	Margaret H.
Catherine C.	Isabelle P.	Maria F.
Channa P.	Jackie O.	Maria S.
Cherlyn F.	Jamie M.	Mary S.
Christina W.	Janne S.	Mashael A.
Christy N.	Jennifer M.	Melanie D.
Corleen C.	Jennifer G.	Meredith L.
Cory L.	Jennifer C.	Michael R.
Courtney D.	Jerry H.	Natalie G.
Crystal H.	Jim S.	Nathalie D.
Cyndi A.	Joey K.	Olga L.
Dana A.	Julie F.	Oli Q.
Deborah L.	Kate M.	Pamela B.

Parvana A.

Pat H.

Paula C.

Ranjani H.

Saghi S.

Sandhya B.

Satya M.

Seth S.

Shannon P.

Shannon C.

Sharon G.

Shawnda M.

Sherrie M.

Simi G.

Sophia S.

Sophie M.

Stacey M.

Steffi D.

Suchada B.

Susan A.

Valerie G.

Van G.

Vanesia A.

Will F.

Xian H.

Ewa B.

LIST OF FIGURES

LIST OF EXERCISES

LIST OF SCRIPTS

NOTES

1 "Why imposter syndrome hits women and women of colour harder," by Sheryl Nance-Nash, Equality Matters, BBC.com, July 27, 2020, https://www.bbc.com/worklife/article/20200724-why-imposter-syndrome-hits-women-and-women-of-colour-harder.

2 "Women in the Workplace 2020," by Sarah Coury, Jess Huang, Ankur Kumar, Sara Prince, Alexis Krivkovich, and Lareina Yee, McKinsey.com, September 30, 2020, https://www.mckinsey.com/featured-insights/gender-equality/women-in-the-workplace-2019.

3 *The Progress Principle: Using Small Wins to Ignite Joy, Engagement, and Creativity at Work*, by Teresa Amabile and Steven Kramer (Harvard Business Review Press, 2011).

4 "12 Little Milestones You Should Be Celebrating at Work," by Stacey Lastoe, The Muse, https://www.themuse.com/advice/12-little-milestones-you-should-be-celebrating-at-work/.

5 *Handbook on Well-Being of Working Women*, edited by Mary L. Connerley and Jiyun Wu (Springer; 1st ed, 2015).

6 *The No Asshole Rule: Building a Civilized Workplace and Surviving One That Isn't*, by Robert I. Sutton (Business Plus, 2007).

7 *Permission to Feel: Unlocking the Power of Emotions to Help Our Kids, Ourselves, and Our Society Thrive*, by Marc Brackett (Celadon Books, 2019).

8 "What Anxiety Does to Us at Work," by Alice Boyes, Harvard Business Review, May 17, 2019, https://hbr.org/2019/05/what-anxiety-does-to-us-at-work.

9 "The Long-Term Effects of Short-Term Emotions," by Dan Ariely, Harvard Business Review, from the magazine (January–February 2010), https://hbr.org/2010/01/column-the-long-term-effects-of-short-term-emotions.

10 "A 3-Step Process to Break a Cycle of Frustration, Stress, and Fighting at Work," by Annie McKee, Harvard Business Review, July 12, 2017, https://hbr.org/2017/07/a-3-step-process-to-break-a-cycle-of-frustration-stress-and-fighting-at-work.

11 "Emotional Intelligence," Psychology Today, https://www.psychologytoday.com/us/basics/emotional-intelligence.

12 *Emotional Intelligence: Why It Can Matter More Than IQ*, by Daniel Goleman (Bantam, 2005).

13 *Emotional Intelligence 2.0*, by Travis Bradberry, Jean Greaves, and Patrick M. Lencioni, (TalentSmart; Har/Dol En 2009).

14 "Emotional Intelligence A Literature Review," by Jensen, Scott & Kohn, Carolynn & Rilea, Stacy & Hannon, Roseann & Howells, Gary, Researchgate publication number 251614532, 2007.

15 "Emotional Intelligence Has 12 Elements. Which Do You Need to Work On?" by Daniel Goleman and Richard E. Boyatzis, Harvard Business Review, 2017, https://hbr. org/2017/02/emotional-intelligence-has-12-elements-which-do-you-need-to-work-on.

16 Exercise recommended to me in a private coaching session with Karin Roest, 2018, https://www.karinroest.com/purposelyfamous.

17 "How to Get the Feedback You Need by Carolyn O'Hara," Harvard Business Review, May 15, 2015, https://hbr. org/2015/05/how-to-get-the-feedback-you-need.

18 "Women in the Workplace 2016," by Lareina Yee, Alexis Krivkovich, Eric Kutcher, Blair Epstein, Rachel Thomas,

Ashley Finch, Marianne Cooper, and Ellen Konar, LeanIn.Org and McKinsey & Company, 2016, https://womenintheworkplace.com/2016#!.

19 "Vague Feedback Is Holding Women Back," by Shelley J. Correll and Caroline Simard, Harvard Business Review, April 29, 2016, https://hbr.org/2016/04/research-vague-feedback-is-holding-women-back.

20 "How Emotional Self-Control Impacts Your Work," by Daniel Goldman and Korn Ferry, https://www.kornferry.com/insights/articles/how-emotional-self-control-impacts-your-work#.

21 "Emotional and Social Leadership Competencies," Key Step Media, https://www.keystepmedia.com/emotional-self-control/.

22 "Staying Calm During an Emergency Can Save Lives," by Gail Gross, July 7, 2016, https://www.huffpost.com/entry/staying-calm-during-an-em_b_7749812.

23 "Five Finger Relaxation Technique," Human Resources Blog of the University of Nebraska-Lincoln, https://hr.unl.edu/five-finger-relaxation-technique/.

24 *Why Zebras Don't Get Ulcers*, by Robert M. Sapolsky (Holt Paperbacks, 2004).

25 "16 Simple Ways to Relieve Stress and Anxiety," Healthline, https://www.healthline.com/nutrition/16-ways-relieve-stress-anxiety.

26 "Hypnosis downloads," https://www.hypnosisdownloads.com/.

27 *Pomodoro Technique Illustrated: The Easy Way to Do More in Less Time*, by Staffan Noteberg (The Pragmatic Bookshelf, 2010).

28 "Productivity 101: An Introduction to The Pomodoro Technique," by Alan Henry, Lifehacker Blog, July 12, 2019, https://lifehacker.com/productivity-101-a-primer-to-the-pomodoro-technique-1598992730.

29 "How a Woman Can Improve Gender Workplace Communication," by Sophie Johnson, Chron, https://work.chron.com/woman-can-improve-gender-workplace-communication-6587.html.

30 *Breaking Through Bias Second Edition: Communication Techniques for Women to Succeed at Work*, by Andrea S. Kramer and Alton B. Harris (Nicholas Brealey, 2020).

31 "13 Reasons Why Meetings Suck & What to do About Them!" by Paul Glover, Fast Company, 2010, https://www.fastcompany.com/1662257/13-reasons-why-meeting-sucks-what-do-about-them.

32   "Influence of Communication Partner's Gender on Language" by Adrienne B. Hancock and Benjamin A. Rubin, *Journal of Language and Social Psychology*, volume 34, issue 1, page(s) 46–64. Article first published online: May 11, 2014; Issue published: January 1, 2015, https://doi.org/10.1177/0261927X14533197.

33   "Why Hillary Clinton Gets Interrupted More than Donald Trump," by Francesca Gino, Harvard Business Review, September 19, 2016, https://hbr.org/2016/09/why-hillary-clinton-gets-interrupted-more-than-donald-trump.

34   "Audience Analysis in Speech and Composition," by Richard Nordquist, ThoughtCo blog, July 12, 2019, https://www.thoughtco.com/audience-analysis-speech-and-composition-1689146.

35   Creating a Good BLUF - Part 1, Manager Tools Podcast, September 2016, https://www.manager-tools.com/2016/09/creating-good-bluf-part-1

36   "Creating a Good BLUF - Part 2," Manager Tools Podcast, September 2016, https://www.manager-tools.com/2016/09/creating-good-bluf-part-2.

37   "Global Talent Trends, 2020," by Mercer, https://www.mercer.com/content/dam/mercer/attachments/private/global-talent-trends-2020-report.pdf.

38 "Are You a High Potential?" by Douglas A. Ready, Jay A. Conger, and Linda A. Hill, Harvard Business Review, June 2010, https://hbr.org/2010/06/are-you-a-high-potential.

39 "The Care and Feeding of High-Potential Employees," by Robert Grossman, SHRM Blog, August 10, 2011, https://blog.shrm.org/workforce/the-care-and-feeding-of-high-potential-employees.

40 "How an Informational Interview Can Boost Your Career," by Alison Doyle, The Balance Careers Blog, August 02, 2019, https://www.thebalancecareers.com/how-an-informational-interview-can-help-your-career-2058564.

41 Khan Academy, https://www.khanacademy.org.

42 "Why are job descriptions so awful?" by Jann Sabin, Medium, Feb 4, 2017, https://medium.com/@soLabis/how-to-improve-your-job-posting-by-88-6dea1942dc2.

43 "Why Women Don't Apply for Jobs Unless They're 100% Qualified," by Tara Sophia Mohr, Harvard Business Review, August 25, 2014, https://hbr.org/2014/08/why-women-dont-apply-for-jobs-unless-theyre-100-qualified.

44 "How to Write a LinkedIn Summary," MIT Career Advising and Professional Development Blog, https://capd.mit.edu/jobs-and-internships/resumes-cvs-cover-letters-and-linkedin/linkedin#summary.

45 "20 steps to a better LinkedIn profile in 2020," by Jane Fleming, LinkedIn, February 20, 2020, https://business.linkedin. com/en-uk/marketing-solutions/blog/posts/content-marketing/2017/17-steps-to-a-better-LinkedIn-profile-in-2017.

46 "10 LinkedIn Profile Summaries That We Love (And How to Boost Your Own)," by Kate Reilly, LinkedIn, July 16, 2019, https://business.linkedin.com/talent-solutions/blog/linkedin-best-practices/2016/7-linkedin-profile-summaries-that-we-love-and-how-to-boost-your-own.

47 "How to Prepare Your Resume (Your Resume Stinks!) (Hall Of Fame Guidance)," Manager Tools Podcasts, October 2005, https://www.manager-tools.com/2005/10/your-resume-stinks.

48 "Interviews - The Introduction," Manager Tools Podcast, October 2006, https://www.manager-tools.com/2006/10/interviews-the-introduction#.

49 "Toyota's Secret: The A3 Report," by John Shook, MIT Sloan Management Review, Summer Magazine 2009, July 1, 2009, https://sloanreview.mit.edu/article/toyotas-secret-the-a3-report/.

50 "The Most Underrated Skill in Management," by Nelson P. Repenning, Don Kieffer, and Todd Astor, MIT Sloan Management Review, Spring 2017 Magazine, March

13, 2017, https://sloanreview.mit.edu/article/the-most-underrated-skill-in-management/.

51 *The Toyota Way: 14 Management Principles from the World's Greatest Manufacturer*, by Jeffrey Liker (McGraw-Hill, 2004).

52 *The A3 Workbook: Unlock Your Problem-Solving Mind*, by Daniel D. Matthews (Productivity Press, 2012).

53 *Developing Leadership Skills 12: Root Cause – Using The 5 WHY'S*, by Jeffrey Liker and George Trachilis (Lean Leadership Institute Publication, 2017).

54 "5 Whys, Getting to the Root of a Problem Quickly," Mindtools blog, https://www.mindtools.com/pages/article/newTMC_5W.htm.

55 *Winning: The Ultimate Business How-To Book*, by Jack Welch and Suzy Welch (HarperCollins e-books; 1st edition 2009

56 *The 4-Hour Workweek: Escape 9-5, Live Anywhere, and Join the New Rich* by Timothy Ferriss, Publisher: Harmony 2009).

57 "Why Women Still Can't Have It All," by Anne-Marie Slaughter, *The Atlantic*, July/August 2012 Issue, 2012. https://www.theatlantic.com/magazine/archive/2012/07/why-women-still-cant-have-it-all/309020/.

58 "37 Tips for a Better Work-Life Balance," by The Muse Editor, The Muse, https://www.themuse.com/advice/37-tips-for-a-better-worklife-balance.

59 "12 Ways to Find More Time in Your Busy Life," by Milena Regos, Thrive Global Blog, https://thriveglobal.com/stories/12-ways-to-find-more-time-in-your-busy-life/.

60 "10 Ways to Create More Time in Your Day," by Lisa Jay, Business Know-how Blog, January 20, 2020, https://www.businessknowhow.com/growth/timetips.htm.

61 "In Pursuit of Work and Life Balance," by F. John Reh, The Balance Careers Blog, updated September 25, 2019, https://www.thebalancecareers.com/work-life-balance-and-juggling-glass-and-rubber-balls-2275864.

62 *Unlimited Power: The New Science of Personal Achievement* by Tony Robbins (Free Press, 1997)

63 *The 5 Love Languages: The Secret to Love that Lasts*, by Gary Chapman (Northfield Publishing, 2015).

64 *Grace-Based Parenting: Set Your Family Free*, by Tim Kimmel (Thomas Nelson Inc, 2005).

65 "Secrets of Body Transformation for Women (free e-course)," Precision Nutrition Blog, https://www.precisionnutrition.com/body-transformation-secrets-women.

66 DAREBEE, an independent global fitness resource, https://www.darebee.com/get-started.html.

67 *Why We Sleep: Unlocking the Power of Sleep and Dreams*, by Matthew Walker (Scribner, 2017).

68 *The Index Card: Why Personal Finance Doesn't Have to Be Complicated*, by Helaine Olen and Harold Pollack (Portfolio, 2017).

69 *The 9 Steps to Financial Freedom: Practical and Spiritual Steps So You Can Stop Worrying*, by Suze Orman (Three Rivers Press, 2000).

70 *The Generosity Factor: Discover the Joy of Giving Your Time, Talent, and Treasure*, by Ken Blanchard and S. Truett Cathy (Zondervan, 2010).

71 Coursera, https://www.coursera.org/.

72 *The Artist's Way: A Spiritual Path to Higher Creativity-25th Anniversary Edition*, by Julia Cameron (TarcherPerigee, 2016).

73 "The VIA Character Strengths Survey," the VIA Institute on Character, https://www.viacharacter.org/.

74 "Here's How Make a Vision Board: Turn your resolutions into a 'crafternoon,'" by Brigitt Earley, O the Oprah Magazine Blog, Nov 26, 2019, https://www.oprahmag.com/life/a29959841/how-to-make-a-vision-board/.

75 "Positive Daily Affirmations: Is There Science Behind It?" by Catherine Moore, Positive Psychology.com, October 13, 2020, https://positivepsychology.com/daily-affirmations/.

76 "Journaling Helped Me Rebuild My Life—Here's How to Start a Practice That Can Help You," by Sophie Gray, Self, January 11, 2019, https://www.self.com/story/how-to-start-a-journaling-practice.

77 Girls Inc., https://girlsinc.org/.

78 Catalyst.org, https://www.catalyst.org/.

79 Society of Women Engineers, https://swe.org/.

Made in the USA
Middletown, DE
20 March 2021